C000139810

E-marketing

WORK THE WEB

E-marketing

SIMON COLLIN

JOHN WILEY & SONS, LTD

Chichester · New York · Weinheim · Brisbane · Singapore · Toronto

Published in 2000 by John Wiley & Sons Ltd,
Baffins Lane, Chichester,
West Sussex PO19 1UD, England

National   01243 779777
International   (+44) 1243 779777
e-mail (for orders and customer service enquiries):
cs-books@wiley.co.uk
Visit our Home Page on http://www.wiley.co.uk
or http://www.wiley.com

Other Wiley Editorial Offices

John Wiley & Sons, Inc., 605 Third Avenue,
New York, NY 10158-0012, USA

WILEY-VCH Verlag GmbH, Pappelallee 3,
D-69469 Weinheim, Germany

Jacaranda Wiley Ltd, 33 Park Road, Milton,
Queensland 4064, Australia

John Wiley & Sons (Asia) Pte Ltd, 2 Clementi Loop #02-01,
Jin Xing Distripark, Singapore 129809

John Wiley & Sons (Canada) Ltd, 22 Worcester Road,
Rexdale, Ontario M9W 1L1, Canada

British Library Cataloguing in Publication Data
A catalogue record for this book is available from the British Library
ISBN-0-471-49897-1

Typeset in 10/12pt Palatino by Dorwyn Ltd, Rowlands Castle, Hants.
Printed and bound in Great Britain by Biddles Ltd, Guildford and King's Lynn.
This book is printed on acid-free paper responsibly manufactured from sustainable
forestation, for which at least two trees are planted for each one used for paper
production.

contents

marketing on the Internet

The Internet provides one of the most effective marketing tools your company can use to promote your brand, service or products. It offers a whole range of new ways to reach new and existing customers, support press enquiries, research campaigns, investigate new export markets, set up focus groups, get advice or discuss techniques with other professionals, or simply find the best place to buy balloons for your next product launch!

In this book, we provide all the latest information you'll need to understand and use the range of new tools available. If you are still planning a start-up or if you're hoping to bring your marketing efforts up to date, we hope you'll find this book a useful starting point. And if you're new to the Internet, flip to the appendix on page 135 for a concise guide to getting your computer – or your office network – online and using all the resources on offer.

Within each chapter, we cover a particular area of marketing and explain how it works on the Net. As well as providing practical information, the book is packed with references to useful websites. All the websites and their addresses are listed by category in the directory at the back of the book.

To bring you up to speed with the opportunities available, here are some of the ways to use the Internet to help you market your company, its brand and products.

direct marketing

E-mail sounds like the perfect marketing tool. It's one of the simplest, but most powerful, ways of reaching customers (or potential customers). And since every other user on the Net has their own unique e-mail address and their e-mail messages pop straight on to their desktop, it's the perfect, most efficient way to reach the target. Or rather it was; unfortunately, almost every other company had the same idea and individuals are getting a bit fed up receiving junk e-mail – just as happened with junk mail through the post.

E-mail provides near-instant delivery, it's almost free and it can be sent as easily to one known individual or 10 000 existing customers. You can send just plain text or you can add in pictures, format your message with colour and typefaces, and add links that take the reader directly to a particular page on your website. It's a great way to provide information on a regular basis, such as:

- sending sales kits or marketing information to distributors and sales reps
- sending press releases to journalists, newspapers and magazines
- announcing new updates or special promotions to existing customers
- sending a regular newsletter or bulletin to keep in touch and improve relations with existing customers.

As in any direct mail campaign, getting the list of addresses is crucial to its success. You can rent a list from a broker or gather addresses yourself. However you get the list, make sure that the people have agreed to receive mail from you – called 'opt-in' users. If you send an advertisement to thousands of unknown people, called spamming, you'll get a stack of flame (rude) messages back, your company will be added to a register of offenders and your Internet provider will probably kick you off its computers.

Because it's such a direct channel to the user, take extra care before you send any marketing material by e-mail. Chapter 8 explains what you can do, how to make the most of e-mail and how to avoid wrecking your company's reputation in the process. Stick to

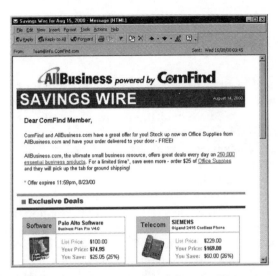

Figure 1.1 Business services website Comfind keeps subscribers up to date with highly formatted, image-rich e-mail newsletters

the guidelines and you'll find that direct e-mail marketing is fast, effective and efficient.

press relations

Press relations are a perhaps surprising benefit of the net. Almost all journalists use e-mail and, acting as intermediaries, there are new virtual press agencies that can distribute your press release to a niche range of reporters. It's quick, efficient and relatively cheap (though the agency will charge a fee). And even the recipients appreciate this development. In Chapter 10, we cover the range of different ways of improving press relations using the Net, from press releases by e-mail to working with reporters on case studies or research for an article.

websites

Your website is your all-day, everyday showroom for your brand and products. You could use it as a simple catalogue that lists and illustrates your products and their benefits – but there's so much more you can do. You can use it to sell products or services in a streamlined, efficient way that requires low overheads and offers convenience for customers. Alternatively, you can use it to provide existing support to your customers or information and reviews for prospective customers.

Your website can include a database of information that's easy to search, multimedia effects, video, sound or even a live link to your office. You can set up sections for journalists or reviewers, and private areas with information for your sales reps or distributors. Or it can be used as an active marketing tool to promote your brand and names in different languages to different export countries. And lastly, you can create an evironment that helps build up a community spirit – with discussion areas, information on your chosen subject, a resource centre and more. In Chapters 3 and 4 we explain how to implement these different features and Chapter 5 discusses how to promote your website to get the most from your resource.

advertising

Just about every commercial website displays advertising banners, the long, oblong strips that tempt visitors to another site. Web-based banner ads are big business – and, if researched and selected carefully, can work as well as traditional ads in the print media. One of the key benefits is that you can reach a precise niche target audience and get precise response figures in return. It's more difficult to do the same with print-based ads.

For example, if you want to advertise a dictionary, find an information website that provides reference material or a language website that appeals to students – both apply to your target customers. Alternatively, you can target potential customers within large, popular search sites (such as Excite or Yahoo!) – both provide the facility to display a particular advertising banner in response to certain search terms typed in by a user. If the user types in 'dictionary', you can ensure that, as well as the search results, the user sees your banner ad.

If the banner ad appeals, the user jumps straight to your website by clicking on the advert. This is precise feedback that's easy to follow and measure. Unfortunately, response rates can be low; users are getting blind to adverts as they spread across the Web. Some users even install special software to remove banner ads from webpages before they are displayed. In Chapter 6 we explain how to plan an online advertising campaign, what to expect from pricing and response rates, and how to design your artwork.

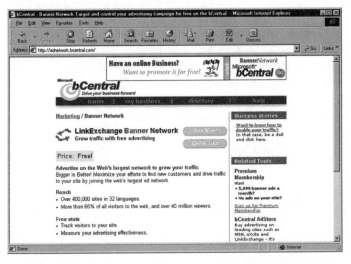

Figure 1.2 LinkExchange at bCentral is one of the biggest free banner ad cooperatives

Alternatively, if you've created a website that's useful, informative and popular with visitors, you could always start to accept banner ads on your site. In Chapter 9, we cover the ways you can sell advertising space, how to implement the mechanics and price the space.

brand marketing

The Internet is a great leveller – small companies have the chance to build up a new brand with the same tools and techniques as the big, brand-oriented multinationals. Some companies use the Net to promote their existing brand, others invent a new E-brand that sounds cool, hip or memorable.

One of the problems of using the Net to promote an existing brand is simply semantics. US-based computer publishing company Ziff Davis (publishers of *PC Magazine*) changed its rather unusual name to the snappier ZDnet, which is also far simpler to spell. At the other end of the scale, Amazon.com has spent its short life promoting its brand as trustworthy and dependable. Now it's one of the first names consumers think of when they shop on the Net; Amazon has taken advantage of this opportunity and has expanded to sell just about anything from books to garden furniture. In Chapter 2 we cover the ways in which you can use the Internet to help plan and implement the branding of your company or product range.

E-commerce

Creating a website that sells things – products or information – provides a useful service to many of your customers. It's partly marketing, partly offering customers the chance to shop for your products when it's convenient for them. If you don't sell online you might be missing an opportunity to serve your customers. Some websites launch as E-commerce sites that are purely replacing high-street shops.

Already there have been casualties in this highly price-sensitive and competitive field. Sites that promote a brand and offer useful and interesting content tend to keep visitors interested for longer – and sneak in a 'buy me' button at the bottom of the page. An alternative take on E-commerce is to sell advertising space on your website.

We cover both ad sales and online shopping in Chapter 9. However, if you are planning an online shop, you'll find more in-depth information in this book's sister title, *E-Commerce*.

response

Response data proves how well any marketing effort is working. On the Net it's easier than ever to record very detailed information about every visitor to your website or person who responds to an advertisement or marketing e-mail.

Just about any action on the Net can be recorded in a log file. Website log files can be analysed to show which particular page is most popular, the route visitors take through your site, even the visitor's country of origin and computer details.

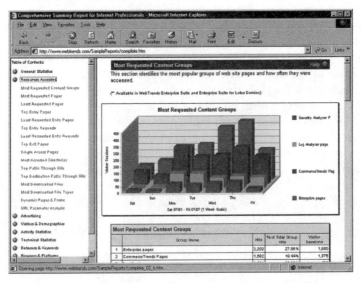

Figure 1.3 Log analysis tools help track visitors to your site and clearly shows the popularity of pages

To help track repeat visitors to your site, you can store tiny scraps of information back to the visitor's own computer, in files called cookies. Some sites store the visitor's name, what they purchased or particular preferences in cookies so that on the next visit, the site can welcome them back by name.

To improve on this basic response analysis, sophisticated geo-targeting software is available that can work with your website to change the information and feedback automatically according to a visitor's particular browsing habits. If the visitor checks the weather in, say, Chicago, the software can start to display local Chicago news stories and adverts. In Chapter 7, we cover the ways to analyse site access logs and implement some of the more sophisticated techniques.

focus groups

Planning a new product or campaign? It's worth testing out a sample or theory on a small focus group of potential customers. This is one way to find out if you've misjudged the price, colour or name before you start production. Up to now, this process was often only used by the biggest companies who could afford to hire specialist agencies. Use one of the new instant-response marketing companies based on the Internet and you'll get the thoughts of hundreds or thousands of selected viewers within minutes – and at a far lower cost.

Alternatively, test out market opinion with the Net's own niche interest groups, provided by newsgroups, mailing lists and discussion groups. You can do much of it yourself if you're careful – very careful – how you tackle the medium. If you plan to do it yourself, make sure that you understand the ground rules – very few groups or mailing lists allow any sort of business message or product plug. Do this and you'll ruin your company's reputation with the group's audience. We cover both these techniques in Chapter 8.

search and research

The Internet is a vast source of data, research material and answers to almost any question. It's a brilliant tool to help research new products, campaigns, monitor your competitors, check patents, compare prices of similar products, estimate potential sales, or even investigate new markets.

In Chapter 11, we cover ways you can use the Internet to help search for data or research a new project. It's easy to get overloaded with information – much of it useless – but it's also astonishingly easy to get hold of information that would take weeks to source any other way. As well as academic and business research, news and data, governments often publish detailed maps of socioeconomic groups within the country, pinpointing areas of particular wealth and key industries. Other official sources provide employment figures, average income and lifestyle guides. All these can help you confirm where to market your products and how to tackle a new market.

buying supplies

Business-to-business (B2B) over the Internet is beginning to take over from business-to-consumer (B2C) commerce, and new websites can help you source supplies more efficiently and at a better price. If you want to get quotes to print a catalogue, visit a specialist B2B website, type in your job requirements and wait for printers to send in bids. Similarly, post requests for prices and service on everything from mailing labels, the supply of embroidered tee-shirts or a new colour photocopier. Use the Directory on page 161, to find sites offering promotional goods, printers, mailing list brokers, and a whole range of other B2B websites ready to supply goods or services.

advice

If you are unsure how to tackle a particular marketing or business problem – and there are no colleagues who can help you out – you could use specialist websites to find articles by experts covering everything from writing a press release to complex branding issues or ensuring e-mail list privacy. If you would rather discuss an idea or problem with other professionals, visit one of the hundreds of discussion groups dedicated to business and marketing. In the Directory on page 159, we list sites such as Wilson Internet (www.wilsonweb.com) that are packed with advice for new and experienced marketing professionals, as well as lists of relevant discussion groups.

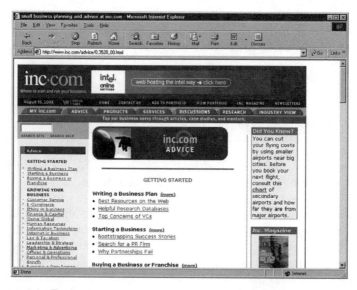

Figure 1.4 Business magazine *Inc.* provides a library of reference pages with advice and guides

strategy

An effective online marketing strategy needs a good plan. It's tempting to try out a few of the techniques as you read this book, but to get a good result you should spend time working out a cohesive plan. This will cover similar techniques to your existing marketing strategy: direct marketing to individuals, brand awareness, press and public relations, research and even product testing. In this section, we'll show you the ways in which you can plan your online assault.

To help you draw up your plan, here are some of the key items you should be considering for your Net-based marketing strategy:

check the finances

Any Internet marketing exercise will cost money. Some tactics are far cheaper than others, some take more time and some will require experts in that field. Throughout the book, we provide guidelines on the cost of implementing each project and any hidden expenses.

brand awareness

Use your existing brand or devise a new E-brand for the networked world. Promote it with your website and other Net marketing work. See Chapter 2 for more information.

direct marketing

Use e-mail to deliver regular messages to existing customers or cold call carefully selected potential new customers. It's cheap, near instant and a lot more convenient than the postal system! See Chapter 8 for more details.

website

Set out your stall with a permanent display of your products and services – available to global customers 24 hours a day. But make sure that your site has interesting, useful content, provides a sense of community and links in to any E-commerce plans your company has set up. Chapter 5 explains how to develop and promote your website.

advertise

The Net is awash with banner advertisements, which appear on just about every commercial website. This strategy can work well to attract potential visitors to your new website, but cost it carefully and be realistic about the often low response rates. See Chapter 6 for details on buying ads.

promote your website

Once you have finished developing your website, spend time carefully promoting it to the search engines and directories on the Web. These vast indexes are the main way visitors will find you among the billions of other pages. See Chapter 5 for details on getting to the top of the index.

participate

The best way to promote your company is to provide good, free advice. Make sure someone identifies and tracks niche newsgroups and mailing lists that cover your company's particular area – answer questions with expert knowledge and leave out the sales pitch – but include a signature with details of your website. See Chapter 12 for details on finding and using newsgroups and mailing lists.

work with the press and media

Streamline your press release delivery by using a virtual e-mail agency to distribute text to niche groups of journalists. Ensure that your website is reporter friendly, with media sections that include company reports, background information, case studies and more to help journalists. Participate in press websites and newsgroups to listen out for requests from journalists.

two

Internet branding

Brand awareness should be an important part of your traditional marketing strategy; on the Net, branding is crucial to a successful commercial site.

One view is that people need not worry too much about branding on the Internet. Market research, for example, shows that the majority of marketing professionals still do not think the Internet is suitable for increasing brand awareness. It is too mass market and sales oriented. One conclusion therefore is that the Web is good for building sales but there's little site loyalty and, with the exception of market leaders like Yahoo! and Amazon, little brand awareness exists. After all, why spend your marketing budget advertising on the Web when rates per view per advert are lower for full-colour ads in a magazine?

There's an opposite view that promotes the web as the perfect medium for branding. Brand awareness and loyalty can be built very quickly, say the proponents of this approach, and Web consumers are desperate for some recognisable names that will help them decide if a site is trustworthy. Users don't just want to spend hours in online shopping sites, they want reliable, information-rich sites rather than a buying spree.

move fast

There's an opportunity available to create and promote your brand on the Web, but you'll need to move fast, since one of the basic ingredients, website domain names, are in short supply. And because the Net is still developing fast, there is plenty of scope to create a powerful brand. With the information provided in this book, you can market your site, your company and your products to good effect. Choose your brand carefully and it's still possible to make a big impact on your Web audience. Using other media, it would take more time, money and effort to move from start-up to recognised brand; the Web, with its instant feedback, provides an immediate reaction.

Every website is referenced by a unique domain name (see the Appendix on page 135, for a primer on how the Net works). Even if your company has a registered name or trademark in the real world, you will still have to re-register for a domain name. For a more professional look, you should register your company's own domain name for e-mail and for your website. For example, if you work at Dan's Coffee Imports, you could have an e-mail address at your ISP (Internet service provider) that reads 'CoffeeImports @compuserve.com' or 'info@coffeeimports.demon.co.uk', but it only takes a little effort to register your own domain and use 'orders@coffeeimports.com'.

Registering your own domain name is very easy, and relatively inexpensive. You can ask your ISP to do this for you or you can do it yourself by visiting a site such as Network Solutions (www. networksolutions.com) or NetBenefit (www.netbenefit.co.uk). (If you've signed up with CompuServe and AOL or almost any of the free ISPs, you'll need to use a second ISP to register and manage your domain name.)

Domain names are being registered at an astonishing rate, so move fast or you'll lose your preferred name. To check if your domain name is still available, use a specialist search tool. Network Solutions (www.networksolutions.com) has a good utility that also helps suggest alternative domain names. Alternatively, visit Great Domains (www.greatdomains.com) to see a list of high-profile names that are up for auction at a premium price.

One final warning: think about the different ways in which your name could be spelt – and register the alternatives. In our example, a visitor might think the domain for Dan's Coffee Imports is 'coffee-imports.com' or 'coffee-imports.co.uk'. A great example of this confusion is the domain name Preztige. Several companies with the same name launched with '.com', '.org' and '.co.nl' endings. One was a pizza delivery service, another a pornographic site and another a gardening service. The confusion was made public and they have all now changed their names. Similarly, 'londongarage.co.uk' is a funky London-based music label, whereas 'londongarage.com' is a smart London-based car showroom.

Even the big names get themselves into a knot. The mega search engine AltaVista started life with the workmanlike domain name of 'www.altavista.digital.com' (when it was supported by computer company Digital). As the brand grew, more visitors started using the service, but it was marketed simply as 'AltaVista'. Another company had registered 'www.altavista.com' and derivatives 'www.digital.altavista.com' and 'www.alta-vista.com' and so on. If you couldn't remember the correct domain, it often took a few attempts to find the site. Thankfully, it's all sorted out and AltaVista, one of the best search engines around, is at www.altavista.com, with a UK-specific edition at www.altavista.co.uk. However, compare this with rival search engine Excite. This has a simpler name and

Figure 2.1 ZDnet provides a clear, effective online brand fronting a library of information, guides and news from its real-world range of computer magazines

started off branding as www.excite.com, www.excite.co.uk and so on – there's no possibility of mistaking the brand.

inventing a brand

To create a strong brand, especially on the Internet, you need a good name. There are a few essentials to choosing a name that works in the wired world – things that wouldn't normally be a worry for traditional brands.

 Is the name short and snappy? Domain names were traditionally fewer than a dozen characters long – even though you can now have domain names several hundred characters long, no one will be bothered to type these in.

 Does the spelling work in different languages and different versions of English? Don't forget you have a global audience – GreatColors might work in the USA, but in the UK the spelling's different.

 Is it easy to spell or will users have no idea how many os or fs are in the name? For example, search engine Ask Jeeves (www.askjeeves.com) changed its global brand to Ask (www.ask.co.uk) – this is simpler to understand and spell, especially since the concept of a famous butler does not work well in other cultures.

 If you must have more than one word in the name, make sure you register derivatives of this, one separated by a dash, one not.

websites

A website markets your company all day and every day. It can be viewed just as easily by a potential customer in the next street as by one on the other side of the world. It lets you advertise your range of products and services and promote your brand, without anyone being physically present with the customer. With some careful planning, you can also provide automated features that supply answers to common questions from customers, product upgrades for existing customers, maps of local stockists, ways to make the most of your products, and customers' glowing reviews. You can also provide shopping features to automate the order-taking and payment process (see Chapter 4), provide areas for press and media information, and even support your reps with online sales kits. And lastly, you can provide a multitude of resources and information that could be useful to a potential browser; if you sell coffee, include information on how it was grown and imported, how to make a perfect espresso or links to sites that sell mugs, biscuits and coffee makers.

However, before you create your killer website, you should take some time to consider and plan how the site will look and how to make best use of all your resources. The site has to look good and be easy to navigate, but the main point to consider is why you are creating it. If you are aiming for a site to raise brand awareness, your design should emphasise the brand logo, message and colours. If yours is a selling site, you'll need to provide a quick, efficient route to finding, selecting and paying for a product.

content and community

Two of the key elements of a successful website are content and community (the third 'C' is commerce). If you have a super-sleek design but nothing to say, people might visit once but won't bother returning. In contrast, sites brimming with useful content will always be popular, regardless of their design.

When you've been browsing the Web, make a note of the sites where you've lingered longer than expected. Some of the most interesting sites provide stacks of extra information, in addition to the basic catalogue of products. For example, Garden.com lists loads of garden equipment, seeds and plants for sale as well as promoting its vast encyclopaedia of garden answers and a rather cool online garden design tool. Similarly, Amazon (www.amazon.com, www.amazon.co.uk and www.amazon.de) lists millions of books, but also provides author news, the chance to contribute your own review of a book and lists of the top titles. Make sure that you provide interesting content, not just a dull catalogue.

Here are some of the most popular ways you can incorporate content and a feeling of community on your website. To add any of these features to your site, you'll probably need to install special software – ask your Web space provider, buy a commercial product or use a free Perl script from ScriptSearch (www.scriptsearch.com).

- Include a section with links to related online resources that visitors might find useful. For example, a book distributor in Milan might include links to the various bookshops in Milan, links to publishers' websites, even information and guides about the city and transport. An estate agent in London might include links to mortgage companies, insurance companies, removals firms, decorators, building trade organisations, local parish groups, travel guides to the area, restaurant maps – anything useful to someone who's considering a move there.
- Provide support for your products, answer common questions online and include tips and tricks to help your customers get the most from your products.

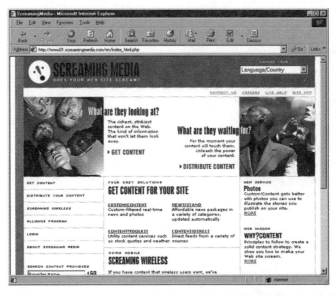

Figure 3.1 Content licensing site ScreamingMedia provides material from a wide range of suppliers

■ Include news headlines from your industry or links to articles and features in magazines. Sites such as ScreamingMedia (www.screamingmedia.com) act as a central broker supplying just about any type of new content.

■ Include a searchable database, if you've got information worth promoting. A site on food and cooking might have a database of recipes or even an online dictionary or glossary. See page 31 for more information about installing a database.

■ Discussion groups add activity to your site with little effort on your part (see Chapter 4 for more on using discussion groups). Visitors can chat among themselves, or ask you for advice or support.

■ Set up a mailing list (often called a list server) and ask visitors to subscribe by entering their e-mail address. You can use the mailing list to distribute a regular newsletter or to provide a forum where subscribers can exchange ideas.

- Include sections on your website with feedback forms that let visitors request further information, send in comments or ask for technical support.
- Include a daily tip or offer of the day – or if you're appealing to a mass market, try a daily syndicated cartoon or weather forecast. See page 37, for content providers.
- A guest book is a simple way of encouraging visitors to leave their comments about your site or products – these can then be read by any other visitor. It's not as interactive as a discussion group, but works well with academic sites.
- Maps are popular – and useful. Almost every hotel website includes an interactive map, often supplied by specialist companies such as MapQuest (www.mapquest.com), that lets a visitor see exactly where the hotel is located.

website design

The design of your website affects the way in which visitors perceive your site, but also how they use it. If your design is rich in images, it'll take an age to display on a user's computer – and they might well have got bored and switched to another site. Alternatively, if the design's a model of sparse white space, they might spend ages trying to find how to navigate around or find information about a particular product.

Unlike the design of a catalogue or advert, webpage designers need to consider the impact on speed of adding images, how to implement special fonts and logos and how to design a structure that's easy to navigate. One of the main problems when designing a website is that you are normally limited to the HTML (hypertext markup language) formatting commands that are used to describe almost all webpages.

Because of the limiting nature of HTML, it's very hard for a designer to place an object in a specific spot on the screen. The language is fine for setting size and alignment of text and, to a certain degree, you can position images and text on a page using tables and

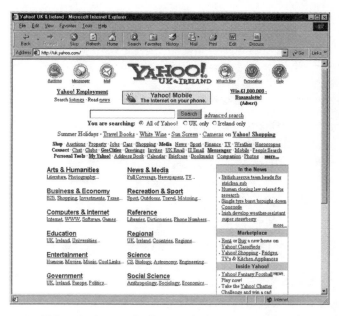

Figure 3.2 Yahoo!'s clear and effective design ensures that the site loads quickly

frames (see later in this chapter), but it is still not as precise as with a DTP page layout application.

Look at some of the most popular websites, such as Yahoo! (www.yahoo.com) and AltaVista (www.altavista.com). Both use a clean, clear design that's simple and relies on text and blocks of colour with just a few, small images. As a result, they display very quickly. Compare this with an image-rich website that can take several minutes to download and display. One of the cruellest but most useful sites for a Web designer is Web Pages That Suck (www.webpagesthatsuck.com), packed with examples of bad Web designs with comments from two top designers.

To produce a good design, you'll need to think how the user navigates the site, how the page looks (on different types of computer) and how long it takes to display. To make things harder, some older version of the user's Web browser software cannot display some design features and the different brands of web browser often display the same page in different ways. Use sites like

Figure 3.3   For a guide to poor design, visit Web Pages That Suck

BrowserWatch (www.browserwatch.com) to see how different browsers are developing.

Here are key points to consider when designing your new website:

- Don't make your visitors wait too long: don't use large graphic images. If you must display a high-resolution image, use a small thumbnail that links to and displays the larger image if the user clicks on it.
- Try not to use too many of the latest HTML layout commands and features that are likely only to work on the newest version of Web browser software. Most visitors will be using older versions and some access the Web by text-only displays.
- Ensure that your site's easy to navigate. Try to include a consistent navigation panel on each page.
- Once the basic structure and design are complete, ask people not involved in the project to try it out and comment.
- Try to provide a clear opening front page and don't be tempted to start off with a full multimedia presentation – as many sites

do. If a visitor simply wants to see if you supply a particular widget, they're unlikely to wait for a five-minute animation and sound track to play.

- Flag any new information available and try to provide an idea of when your site was last updated. No one wants to read old news. If the information rarely changes, add a little dynamic content, possibly through a discussion group. If this does not fit into the design, simple tricks such as displaying today's date near the logo – as do Amazon.com and Excite – at least give the impression that the site is relevant today.
- Include plenty of links within the text to other sections on your site.
- If you have lots of products or information, provide a simple search tool that can find the page without tedious navigation.
- Look at how the most successful sites – and your favourite sites – have designed their pages. Print out a copy of their opening page and identify the elements that make it easy to use, friendly and informative – then try to incorporate these into your design.
- Ensure that there's plenty on offer, but don't pack everything into the opening page.
- Use fonts and colours with care. Try to keep a consistent palette of colours and use just one font with different sizes and styles for impact.

using a Web design company

You can create your own sophisticated, feature-packed website for next to nothing – if you're prepared to do all the work yourself and learn about basic programming and coding skills. However, most companies have neither the time nor the programming and design expertise to plan and implement a basic site, let alone something as complicated as an interactive E-commerce online shop. If you want to put up a simple catalogue site with pictures of your products and services, you can buy a webpage design package (see the Directory, page 147, for details) and create a basic, but nonetheless effective presence on the Web. The costs should be around £100 for the software (although some are free) and a monthly rental fee of about £10 for Web space where you can publish your site.

If you don't mind spending time and effort learning about page design, you'll find it interesting and productive. However, most companies would prefer to stick to their own area of expertise and instead turn to a specialist Web design company with which they can work to plan the structure and design of their site. This is especially important if you want to set up an online shop or complex database-driven service.

Web design companies normally work on a per-project fee basis; once you have both agreed a basic structure and provided sample material that should be included in the site, you'll get an estimate of the time and costs required. This can vary from a few thousand up to several hundred thousand pounds. However, perhaps the biggest problem is trying to find a Web design company that produces something you like. Specialist Web business magazine sites normally include directories of design companies; try *Internet.Works*

Figure 3.4 *Internet.Works* magazine provides a directory of Web design companies around the UK

(www.iwks.com) or *Business 2.0* (www.business2.com). Next time you are browsing on the Net, make a note of the sites you think are well designed and effective in promoting their message – you'll normally find a credit to the design company that developed the site somewhere on the home page.

When you're commissioning a Web design company, try to work out a way in which you can update material directly, without having to pass it back through the design company. This will ensure that you keep the site up to date without incurring offputting service charges.

your address

When you sign up with any Web space provider – or your ISP (Internet Service Provider) – you'll get an allocation of Web space where you can publish your website. This space has its own unique address, normally called its URL (uniform resource locator), which lets any other user find and view your site. To start with, your URL is normally made up of the service provider's name and your user name. For example, if a company called Coffee Imports signed up with Demon Internet, their address could be 'www.coffeeimports.demon.co.uk'.

This URL is enough to get you started: any other user can type in the address and view the pages; you can submit the address to search engines and print it on your letterhead. However, it doesn't look very professional. For around £50 most ISPs will register your own domain name and link this to your Web space at your service provider. And if you're still wavering, here are two other points worth considering: it doesn't say much for your professional image if you promote a website on a free ISP such as Freeserve; secondly, domain names are running out so you should register now before someone else gets the same idea.

To get a website address that doesn't feature the service provider's name, you'll need to register your own domain name. To continue with our example, 'www.coffeeimports.co.uk' might be a good home for our company. The simplest way to register your own domain name is to ask your Internet provider to do the work for you. You'll have to pay an initial registration fee, then a yearly subscription just to maintain your domain name (it's normally between £40 and £100 per year). If you want to register the name yourself, visit one of the main registration services such as Network Solutions (www.network solutions.com) or NetBenefit (netbenefit.co.uk).

Once you have your domain name, it will refer to your website and to your e-mails. In our example, we would receive any mail sent to the domain, for example 'orders@coffeeimports.co.uk', and visitors would see our website by typing in 'www.coffeeimports.co.uk'.

If you're stuck trying to think of a domain name for your company because your first choice has already been registered, try using the nifty device at Network Solutions (www.networksolutions.com) – type in words that describe your business or brand and it will combine them into a list of possible names.

how do you build it?

A website is made up of individual webpages that each contain certain elements: text, graphic images, and perhaps an advanced feature such as an order form or database search panel. Even if you plan to use an external Web design agency, it's worth getting to grips with the way in which webpages are designed, if only to understand how the agency is working and what is (and is not) possible to implement.

Behind almost every webpage is a special set of codes, called HTML (HyperText Markup Language), that tell the Web browser software how to format and display the text and image links within the webpage. In the old days, you would have to learn the hundreds of HTML codes before you could create a webpage. Now, the coding process is almost entirely hidden away behind sophisticated page design software. Using a design program is similar to using a desktop publishing (or sophisticated wordprocessor) software. Type in text, format and change the fonts, add in images, create links, add animation and create response forms without seeing any HTML code.

If you want to experiment with ideas, you'll find that the most flexible and powerful way is to use a special webpage design program such as Microsoft FrontPage (www.microsoft.com), Fusion NetObjects (www.netobjects.com) or Adobe Dreamweaver (www.adobe.com) – but these can take a while to learn how to use. Most Web design (also called page authoring) software is sold as commercial products, but you can download trial versions that will run for 30 days before you have to pay. Visit Builder (www.builder.com), WebMonkey (www.webmonkey.com) or Tucows (www.tucows.com) to download time-limited demos of some of the best programs on offer.

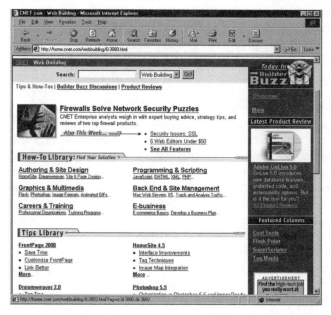

Figure 3.5   The Builder website offers stacks of guides, advice and tips for anyone creating a site

However, to start experimenting, you can use your word-processing software, such as Word or WordPerfect or one of the free simple page design programs supplied with both Microsoft's Internet Explorer and Netscape's Navigator Web browsers.

However, these methods produce very basic pages and you'll find it impossible to create and manage a large business site with a wordprocessor!

advanced features

It's relatively easy to create a website with text, images and links. The design can be clean, simple or complex, but the content remains basic text and pictures. If these two elements are good enough, the site should start to attract visitors. However, to keep them on your site you will probably need to add extra, more advanced features to provide discussion groups, a searchable database or an online catalogue. These advanced features are normally carried out by a custom-written program running on your ISP's server computer.

You'll often see these advanced programs referred to as CGI (common gateway interface) scripts. CGI refers to a path relating the webpage front to the advanced feature and the program running on the server that carries out the action.

Most of the programs that run on Web servers to provide these advanced features, such as shopping carts, quizzes or databases, have been created using a programming language called Perl. You could learn Perl and write your own programs – it's not too complicated, but it is still a challenge for non-programmers. Visit the Perl archives (www.perl.org) for information and help. An alternative is to visit one of the vast libraries of free and shareware programs written in Perl by other programmers. SuperScripts (www.superscripts.com), ScriptSearch (www.scriptsearch.com) and FreeCode (www.freecode.com) have hundreds of finished programs that you can copy and use to enhance your website. It sounds ideal, but it can take days to get one of these Perl programs working properly on your site.

The last alternative is to use a commercial or custom-written solution. Some applications – notably database design – have a good range of commercial off-the-shelf solutions (such as Filemaker Pro, Oracle and Access) or you can pay a programmer (or Web design

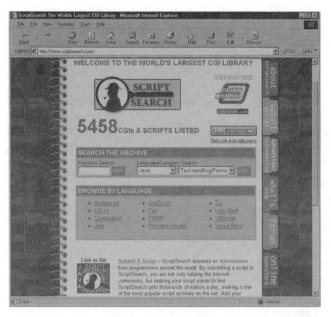

Figure 3.6 Find Perl scripts, the most common way of adding advanced features, in a library like ScriptSearch

company) to create and install a custom program for your requirements. See the Directory, page 147, for a range of sites that will help you get started on adding programs and advanced features to your site.

adding a database to your site

A database provides a simple interface to a mass of information, allowing visitors to your site to search for and display a particular entry of interest. If you've looked for a book on Amazon (www.amazon.com) or tried to find a cheap computer on Jungle.com (www.jungle.com), you have been searching a database. As well as these commercial applications, there are thousands of non-commercial sites that use a database to manage their data – for example Scoot (www.scoot.co.uk) lets you search for a company's contact details by name or location, and TheBiz (www.thebiz.co.uk) lets you search its files for a particular business website.

To add a database to your website you could use a free Perl script, although as already explained this is not an easy process. Alternatively, you could use a specialist webpage design program such as Microsoft FrontPage, which has database support built in to let you add a Microsoft Access database to your website with a few clicks (but needs special FrontPage features configured by your Web space provider). Or you could use a stand-alone commercial database product such as FileMaker Pro (www.filemaker.com) – that again requires support from your Web space provider. If you plan on adding any of these advanced features, you'll find it useful to talk to your hosting company; it might support one of these solutions or have a different solution available. See the Directory, page 148, for details of database providers.

getting Web space

If you want the rest of the Internet world to be able to view your website, you'll have to publish the individual pages that you have designed on a public Web server. This means buying – or, more usually, renting – space on a server computer's hard disk where your files can be stored. Once you publish your website, each page will have its own unique address. To start with the address will probably include your ISP's name, but you can register your own domain name and point this to your webpages (your ISP can do this for you). Once you have done this, any visitor typing in your domain name will automatically view the webpages you have published.

To publish your website, you have to copy all the individual files (those that make up each page, together with any images, program scripts and database files) to the area of Web space on your ISP or virtual server's computer. Once the files are on the public server, anyone on the Internet will be able to view the site. All the main webpage design programs (including FrontPage, NetObjects and

Figure 3.7 The FilemakerPro database software provides a simple way to design and publish a Web database

Dreamweaver) include a function that will automatically copy all the files directly to your Web space.

The simplest way to get Web space is to ask your ISP: it probably already provides you with a certain amount of free Web space. Almost every ISP (including those that are free) will supply you with Web space as part of your account. However, if you use a free ISP (such as Freeserve or Virgin Net), you may pay nothing, but you cannot easily have your own domain name, set up a complex database or include other advanced features. ISPs that charge for their services also provide Web space and you are generally offered a range of extra features, from associating a domain name with your website to design and E-commerce.

A popular way to get cheap Web space and a lot of extra features is to sign up with a company that only offers Web space – it doesn't provide telephone access numbers, but instead specialises in renting out space on its servers for your website. These companies, called hosting providers or virtual servers, don't have to spend their money on expensive telephone equipment to provide users with access to the Net so generally offer good value for money. However, if you decide to use a virtual server, you'll also need a standard ISP just to connect to the Internet – although any ISP, even a free one, will work.

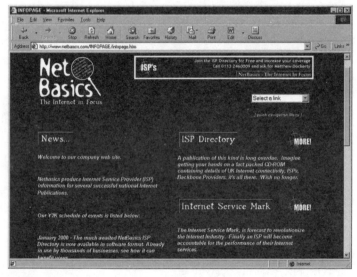

Figure 3.8 Use a rating service to check if your prospective ISP offers reliability and speed

If your website is particularly complex, displays real-time information (such as the level of your warehouse stock) or attracts a huge number of visitors, you might consider installing your own server. You avoid using an ISP or virtual server company to manage the computer, but you will need an expert to install and maintain the hardware, software and network connections to the Internet. A mid-way option is to rent a complete computer (rather than just a section of hard disk space) that is located at a specialist ISP's headquarters. This gives you the flexibility to install your own custom-written software and near limitless storage capacity.

Best of all, you do not have to worry about managing or maintaining the complex network connections. This type of installation – called a co-located server – is a popular choice for companies that have complex software and need more features than a standard service can offer.

content

If you want a successful website, you need to provide interesting content to attract visitors. This can vary greatly according to the type of website, but it should be useful, interesting and – ultimately – encourage repeat visits from the user. If you have an online E-commerce site (a shop), your content is your catalogue of products, so you need a wide or unique range of products, low prices or great service to compete with the other online shops. Some shops add information and other content, such as reviews of products (see Amazon.com) or discussion forums. If you have an information-only based site, you might attract visitors because of your lively discussion group, up-to-date news (trade or product news rather than world news) or tips and tricks that visitors won't find on other sites. In short, the aim of building a content-rich website is to convince your visitors that your site is packed with useful information and is worth visiting on a regular basis.

To encourage repeat visits from Net browsers, you'll need to involve them in as many ways as possible. Create an environment that is dynamic and relevant – this will take time and effort to set up and manage, but the access figures should start to reflect the increased number of visitors and provide better exposure for your site. Best of all, these repeat visitors are not just passing surfers but are regular visitors who have built up a trust in your company and the service you offer.

There are three types of content that you can provide to visitors, based on the fundamental three 'C's of commerce, content and community.

First is commerce: if you have a Web-based online shop, you are providing a reason for visitors to come and visit your site. If your shop is the same as all the others, there's little reason to stay and visitors might migrate to a better-known or more established shop. However, if you offer low prices, a unique range of products or great back-up and support, then passing browsers might stop and shop.

The second attraction is pure content: this means information that you provide for the benefit of the visitors. For example, you might include the latest news headlines, weather reports, a dictionary, games, or reference guides to making the most of a product. You could include a real-time share price feed for your company or sector, or television schedules, sports results and commentary to attract and keep visitors.

Figure 4.1 Almost every website, including giants such as MSN, licenses content

Third is community: you provide features on your site that let visitors create their own community and generate interesting content. If you set up a discussion group relating to your products or your industry, you might attract visitors that want to read the latest messages – but if the chat is slow and dull, you might frighten off more users than you attract.

Feedback forms ensure that visitors can let you know how they feel about your products – far better than providing no feedback mechanism and leaving disgruntled customers to vent their frustration in a public newsgroup. An online shop lets you create a new outlet for your products, dedicated all day and every day to promoting your services.

Or why not create a resource page that includes a library of links to other sites of interest to your visitors – and provide an add-a-link feature so that they can contribute worthwhile sites. Linking a database lets users search custom data, from classifieds to guide books, product news to support tips.

If you want to build a community feeling into a site, consider a calendar feature to provide online diaries of conventions or even personal calendars for each visitor. Some companies – such as estate agents and car manufacturers – use multimedia walk-throughs to demonstrate a house or new model through sound and video.

All of these methods of adding content to your site are ways to make your website 'sticky' – to keep visitors browsing on your site as long as possible. This is particularly important if you plan to sell banner ad space (see Chapter 9) or if you want to sell a product or service. The sites that fail are those that attract visitors with great advertising or a unique concept, but then fail to deliver enough interesting content – to use Net-speak, they're not sticky.

Your aim when creating a user-friendly website is not just to create an online version of your catalogue. That's too easy and too dull. Visitors will drop by the site, have a quick look at your products and move on. The real trick is to create a place that not only encourages the visitor to drop in, but then provides enough material for them to stay a while.

Some of the most interesting sites provide more extra related information than actual core-product details. For example, the Amazon.com site (www.amazon.com) lists millions of books, but also provides author news, the chance to contribute your own review of a book and lists of the top titles. You can easily visit there looking for a book and end up spending an hour browsing book-related information. Have another look at your site's structure: are you providing a catalogue or an information-rich experience?

To add content and community to your site, below are some of the tools that you can use to get started and the issues to consider. To

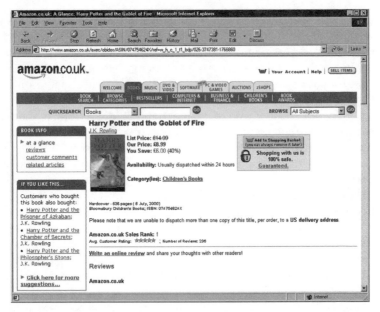

Figure 4.2 Amazon lets visitors add reviews to books as one way of keeping visitors on its site

add an E-commerce element to your site, look for an overview in Chapter 9 or refer to the sister book in this series, *E-Commerce*.

licensing content

Setting up a content-rich website used to be difficult – and expensive. If you wanted to add information such as news, reviews, weather or even financial information to your site you had to hire a team of editors or pay high licensing fees to different information providers.

Now, you can use your expertise to concentrate on your own niche subject and license any other material you need from one of the new breed of one-stop content markets. One of the biggest is ScreamingMedia (www.screamingmedia.com), which provides a central point where you can find content from hundreds of different information providers – from magazines to financial data, weather to sports results. Most of the information is updated by the providers on a daily or even real-time basis and is available to license for a modest fee. Simply choose the type of information you want, select from the range of suppliers listed and pay the licence fee; you add a special line of code to your website that pulls fresh information from the provider's computer each time your website is visited, ensuring that the content is always up to date.

multilingual considerations

One of the first points to get right – and one that most developers leave until last – is the language issue. This is growing rapidly in importance as the number of non-English-speaking users rockets. The majority of Internet users are still based in the USA, but the rest of the world is getting online fast and demands local-language considerations. The best way to involve non-English-speaking visitors is to provide different language versions of your site or, ideally, localized sites for each main country in your territory.

The first consideration is to provide translations of your Web text. If you have an in-house translation department, make sure that it realises the limitations of webpage design – roman characters with accents, as used in much of western Europe and the US, can be represented very easily on the Web, but different scripts, such as Cyrillic or Japanese, need special font files to be installed on the user's computer.

Many translation agencies have switched to a specialised, and lucrative, service of translating webpages. To find a specialist, use a translation job exchange such as Aquarius (www.aquarius.net) or search the Languages: Translation section of Yahoo.com. Alternatively, try an automatic service such as the one offered by AltaVista (www.altavista.com) – simply visit that site and click on the 'translate' button to get an instant, if often very rudimentary, translation.

To make your website seem local to a country, consider registering a local domain name that can be pointed to a particular section

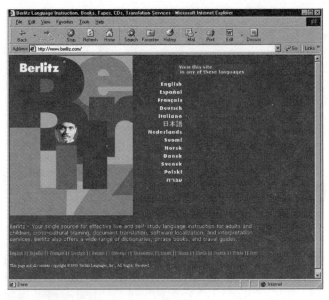

Figure 4.3   Language school chain Berlitz expects visitors from around the world and offers multilingual versions

of your main website. For example, the .com suffix was originally used to indicate a US-based commercial organisation, but can now be used by any international organisation. A .co.uk suffix shows a UK site (or localised UK site), similarly with .co.jp for Japan and so on.

discussion groups

Discussion groups are a good way of adding community to your website – and best of all, once they have regular active visitors, they require little effort on your part. Instead, it's the visitors who contribute to the discussion group and can ask a question or reply to another user's query. When a discussion group becomes popular, it can generate hundreds or thousands of messages per day and attract visitors who want to catch up on the latest messages. After you have set up the discussion group features, you need to work hard initially to promote this forum and prevent it drying up.

Figure 4.4 Discussion groups are an important feature of personal finance site Motley Fool

Visit successful discussion groups on sites such as Raging Bull (www.ragingbull.com) or Motley Fool (www.fool.com) to see how the concept works in practice. Any visitor can submit a message; this is stored on your Web server with a title. For example, a user on Motley Fool (a financial information site) might want to ask other users' opinions on the value or prospects of a particular share. They simply type in their message in a form displayed on the site and click 'submit'. The new message will be stored and listed in the main group of messages. If another user reads this and wants to reply, they highlight the message from the list and click 'reply'. Their new message now appears as an adjunct to the original. After some activity on your board, the message structure will look like a tree with original messages and branches off these for replies.

To set up a discussion group (sometimes called a bulletin board), you'll need to acquire, install and configure special software that runs on your Web server. For most websites, this means installing the software on the computer where you publish your webpages – typically your ISP or Web space host.

Some Web space providers will include pre-configured discussion groups as a free add-on feature in your package. However most don't, so you will need to install your own software. Discussion group management software is normally written as a script in the Perl programming language (so it can work on almost every Web server). You'll find some commercial products that are offered for a fee, but most are offered as freeware or shareware within software libraries such as ScriptSearch (www.scriptsearch.com) or FreeCode (www.freecode.com). See the Directory, page 148, for details of software libraries and discussion group software developers.

Installing a Perl script is complex, unless you are experienced with this type of program. You normally need to set up the name and title of the group together with any security restrictions and the name of a moderator. Once you have done this, you can copy the files to your Web server (upload them using a system called FTP, similar to the way webpages are copied to the Web server). If you're unsure, ask your ISP or Web space provider to help or give you instructions. Finally, once the main control software is installed and running, you'll need to design a set of webpages that work with the software and let visitors post a new message or reply to an existing one.

guest books

One of the simplest – if now rather old-fashioned – ways to encourage users to comment on your site or products is to provide an electronic guest book. This lets your visitors tell you, and other visitors, about themselves and their opinions. It's a feature that's popular on hobby and academic sites, but is perhaps best replaced with a discussion group (where you can answer back) if you supply services or expect problems. If you want to add a guest book, you'll find plenty of free Perl scripts to download from libraries such as ScriptSearch (www.scriptsearch.com) and FreeCode (www.freecode. com) – but you'll need some experience in the Perl programming language to install the software quickly and efficiently.

link directories

It might seem perverse to provide links to other websites within your own site, especially if you have spent time and effort getting visitors on to your site. However, a directory of links to related or interesting sites can be a useful attraction in its own right. The biggest search engines, such as Yahoo! (www.yahoo.com) and About (www.about.com), started as small directories of links to interesting sites on the Web.

To keep it simple, you could have a basic webpage that only you can add to and change, listing useful rather than competitive sites. Alternatively, you could install a special directory software program (there are several free and shareware products to download at ScriptSearch and FreeCode) that let you build a service just like Yahoo!'s famous directory. You will need some experience in Perl to install the software on your Web server and then patience to fill up the directory with entries and descriptions. However, once it has begun to grow, you'll find that visitors might even use this as their starting point rather than a bigger, well-known search engine. A good example is TheBiz (www.thebiz.com), which started as a basic directory of business sites online and now includes thousands of useful business sites, information and news.

databases

Adding a database to your website is one of the most popular ways of providing a useful service and attraction – so long as the database is filled with something of interest! The data could be as varied as a telephone directory – such as Yellow Pages (www.yell.co.uk) – or your vast collection of recipes featuring your products – such as Foodoo (www.foodoo.com). Users can search for information using a special search form; you need to install and configure software to carry out the search on your database, then format and display the results on a webpage.

Almost every major website has some form of database. Some are complex systems, such as the complete Yellow Pages telephone directory (at www.yell.co.uk in the UK and www.bigyellow.com in the US). Other custom sites include the *AutoTrader* classified car magazine (www.autotrader.co.uk) that lets you search for a car by make, model and price. Larger sites organise their product support databases to let visitors search for tips or answers based on a product or problem.

If adding a database sounds a good idea, you need to plan the installation carefully. See the Directory, page 147, for details of software that you'll need for carrying out the search process. Many business-oriented ISPs provide expertise to install a database and manage the programming required – for a fee. Some website management tools, notably Microsoft Frontpage (www.microsoft.com) and FileMaker Pro (www.filemaker.com), allow you to integrate a database directly into the website design; however, the ISP needs to install special control software to support these features.

A popular method of adding a database is to use one of the many free Perl scripts available from a library such as ScriptSearch or Freecode to manage and search the database. In fact, both these libraries are themselves examples of simple databases.

Lastly, many business-oriented ISPs provide pre-configured search engines that you can use within your website. Many use the same search engine that is employed on the vast Excite search engine (www.excite.com) to provide a personal search engine for your site.

newsletters and mailing lists

A mailing list (often called a list server) is an efficient way to distribute information to a group of users. If you want to send out a regular newsletter, you can use a mailing list to deliver the issue. However, these are normally used to distribute comments by any member of the group to all the other members in the group (see Chapter 8 for more information). It could be a useful addition to your site if you want to promote a community or distribute information to your distributors, clients or salesforce. The one disadvantage of a mailing list is that although you are involving the user and reminding them about your brand or service, they do not actually have to visit your website except for the initial subscribtion phase.

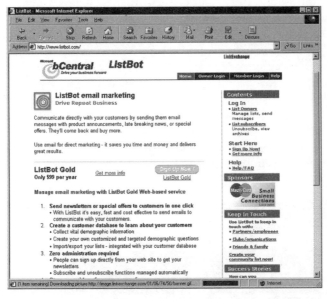

Figure 4.5   Manage a mailing list automatically with the ListBot service

There are two ways to add a mailing list feature to your site. The first is to use one of the many specialist sites that offer this service for free – for example eGroups (www.egroups.com) or ListBot (www.listbot.com); these free services normally add in a line of advertising at the end of each message. The alternative is to set up your own list server on your Web server.

The way a mailing list server works is simple: an application on the server holds a list of the e-mail addresses of subscribers, and when a user submits a new article it is distributed by the mail list server to all the other subscribers in the list. There are plenty of extra features that allow articles to be checked by a moderator before they are mailed out, but this is the basic function. One of the most popular programs is LISTSERV from L-Soft (www.lsoft.com). This software runs on most Web server platforms, but it is far easier to ask your Internet service provider to include this feature in your hosting package. Alternatively, there are dozens of free and shareware programs to download from software libraries such as ScriptSearch and Freecode.

maps

A popular feature on many business websites is an interactive map. Hotels use these to show potential visitors where the hotel is located, estate agent sites use maps to show a particular street or house, Yellow Pages-style phone directories use maps to show the location of a business. And some business sites include a map to help anyone trying to find their office. More obvious users include

Figure 4.6 Map supplier MapQuest licenses its detailed interactive maps to a wide range of sites

travel sites, such as Excite travel (www.excite.com), Yahoo travel (www.yahoo.com) and Expedia (www.expedia.com), who all provide travellers with an instant map of an area to show where to find hotels, restaurants and attractions.

If you want to add a map to your site, you can draw and scan in a simple map as an image. However, this is static and rather dull. More interesting, for the visitor, are interactive maps that let you zoom in on detail, pan from side to side or even type in a postcode and view the street-level location. However, you need original map data and a lot of computing power to manipulate and plot the graphical information. A simpler solution is to license a map feature from one of the specialists, such as MapQuest (www.mapquest.com).

chat servers

Discussion groups (see earlier in this chapter) are relatively passive content providers – a user posts a message then waits (sometimes for days) before they get a reply. The alternative is to set up a chat server. This provides a way for two or more visitors to your site to 'chat' – anything one types is immediately displayed to the other, who can reply. Unlike discussion groups, there's usually no record of what's said; instead it's just a forum to meet or talk to other visitors, or to someone from your company. Websites aimed at teenagers – such as Girrl.com (www.girrl.com) – have dozens of different chat sections where visitors can talk to distant friends or make new chums. Other sites sometimes use chat features to host a talkback forum between a celebrity or representative of the company and any visitor.

Hosting a chat server can be more difficult than many of the other features mentioned in this chapter. You can use a free Perl script – from ScriptSearch or FreeCode – or you can ask your ISP to set up a solution for you. Alternatively, you can use one of the specialist commercial software products on the market, which can also support audio or video presentations, for example ichat (www.ichat.com) and Proxicom (www.proxicom.com).

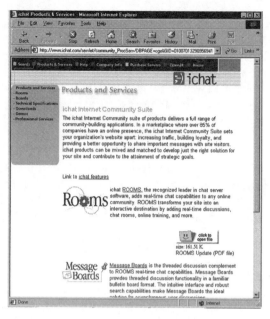

Figure 4.7 Interactive chat from ichat provides a way of adding content and community

Moving one step up in complexity, you could set up a video or audio transmission – particularly popular for live broadcasts of pop bands, celebrity interviews or Web-cams. Many companies use the live sound transmission to broadcast radio over the Web – you can listen to almost any commercial radio station over the Net via vTuner (www.vtuner.com). Some companies use this medium to broadcast a video and sound interview with a president or CEO to reporters or key customers. Or, for the brave (given its moderate quality and often patchy reliability), you could demonstrate a new product to key accounts or journalists via a live video link.

Established technologies such as RealAudio (www.real.com) provide excellent real-time audio and video delivery from a website and are often used to broadcast live radio, concerts or interviews over the Net. Other developers have similar technologies, including Microsoft's NetShow (www.microsoft.com), Netscape MediaServer (www.netscape.com), Macromedia (www.macromedia.com) and Vivo (www.real.com/vivo/).

calendars

Websites promoting a community approach often include an online calendar. This could be created simply to display dates of conferences, holidays or other specific information. A more interactive approach would be to include a personal calendar feature for each user, who can then set up and add their own appointments, reminders and holiday details. It's also a great way of providing an open working environment for teleworkers or travelling colleagues to check diaries and appointments over the Net.

A business site might include a calendar set to display key dates or release schedules to visitors. The system would be driven by a simple Perl program running on the Web server (though for very simple calendars, you could manually edit a webpage each day). The important dates for conventions or product release would be added by the Webmaster or marketing department.

A more active calendar feature lets you and your visitors add or view diary entries – and choose who else can see the diary. Some of these more complex scripts are available from freeware or shareware libraries such as ScriptSearch or FreeCode, or you can use a commercially available product such as Lotus Notes (www.lotus.com), Netscape Calendar (www.netscape.com) or Microsoft's Exchange product (www.microsoft.com).

feedback forms

So far, all the features that we have discussed to provide content provide ways of passing information to your visitors. Don't forget that they might well want to tell you something! Add a page on your site that encourages feedback – provide an e-mail address for visitor comments and a special form on which visitors can type comments that are then sent directly to you.

Creating a feedback form is relatively easy if you are designing your webpages using a graphical page design tool, such as Microsoft FrontPage or NetObjects Fusion. You can draw in a text box, define radio buttons or checkboxes and create a button to submit this information. Once you have designed the form and webpage, you need to set up a special Perl script that runs on your Web server and ensures that what is typed on a form is then sent, normally by e-mail, to a named contact. Most ISPs provide this basic program (often called a formail script) with their Web space package.

promoting
your site

Every day, several hundred new websites are launched to add to the millions already on the Web. Against this vast mass of existing competition, you need to work hard to ensure that your website gets noticed by your target visitors. As well as telling your traditional contacts – including press, and existing and potential customers – you need to consider all the specialist sections of the Net, such as the online search engines that help users find information.

In fact, the key to a successful launch is largely down to the time you spend promoting its profile with the major search engines such as Yahoo! and AltaVista. Once you've attracted visitors, the site will live or die by its content (see Chapter 4).

Here's a checklist of the marketing tasks you'll have to carry out to ensure that your site gets noticed:

- Prepare your webpages by including indexing information for search engines.
- Submit your site to the main search engines.
- Submit your site to the major online review and what's new sites.
- Ask relevant trade organisations if they will include a link to you from their site.
- Use search tools and your access logs to find related websites and ask them for reciprocal links.
- Ask local government-sponsored business sites for a reciprocal link.
- Make sure that the new site address is on company advertising and stationery.

- Modify any e-mail or newsgroup signatures to show your new Web address.
- Research banner advertising to increase exposure.
- Keep newspapers, magazines and agencies informed with a press release.
- Inform key customers and distributors and keep them informed with a regular newsletter.
- Identify and monitor relevant newsgroups and post low-key informational replies.
- Monitor relevant mailing lists and post low-key informational messages.
- Look at using targeted e-mail lists for direct publicity to increase visitors.

The aim of good website promotion is to ensure that your website is always crowded with visitors – once they are on the site, they can decide if they like it, if it's useful or worth revisiting or bookmarking. Use the information in this chapter to ensure that your site has good coverage and gets off to a great start. If you are relaunching or redesigning your site, you should use the same basic steps. But don't do any of this until your site is ready to accept visitors – if they flock on to a construction site, they're unlikely to return.

the search engines

Perhaps the single most important step in marketing your website is to make sure that it's correctly registered with the main search engines and directories (see also Chapter 11 on how to search effectively). These search engines spend their time maintaining their index of millions of websites, each with a short description and link to the site. You know how they work – you've probably used them to find a site – if you type in a word, they'll display any websites that match.

Most of the major search engines use automatic software robot programs, called spiders, to find new websites. These sites are analysed and added automatically to the main index. You could wait for the spider to find your new site, but there are so many new sites

Figure 5.1 Each major search engine has a section where you can manually add your new site's details

it could take them weeks to reach yours. Sidestep the automatic system and register your site directly with the search engine.

There are two ways of registering your website with a search engine: you can visit the search engine and manually fill out an electronic registration form, or you can use an automated program to do this work for you across all the search engines. Visiting each search engine yourself takes time, but lets you enter exactly the information you want to appear on the search index. If you use an automated program to do the work, it will ask you once for short and long descriptions of your site and submit these to the search engines. You cannot then tailor the information to each index, but it does save a lot of time! See the Directory, page 149, for a list of the main submission sites that will help promote your site.

Almost all of the automated registration sites charge a fee to submit your site to the 300-odd main search engines on the net (in fact there are thousands of small search and directory sites with which you could register). But most registration sites will normally provide a free service in which your site's details are sent to a number of the top search engines. However, before you register your website with any search engine, to help ensure you get the most from the opportunity, you should make sure that each page on your site has the extra information that is used to help the search engine correctly index the site.

make your site search-engine friendly

To ensure that your website is correctly indexed by the search engines, you can give a helping hand by providing key information, as you would like it presented, rather than rely on the indexing software to analyse and check on your site. If you don't do this step, the search engines will simply use the first few sentences of text in each page and could categorise and summarise your site in a way that's useless for a surfer.

page title
The first step is to ensure that each page on your site has a clear, meaningful page title. You create this with your webpage design software or, if it does not allow this, use a text editor to add in the <TITLE> . . . </TITLE> line near the start of the webpage (with the page title inside these HTML tags).

For most of the pages within your site, you can include your company name, if it's short, but otherwise concentrate on describing the contents of the page. However, for your main home page (normally stored in the index.html file), make sure that you do include your company name in the page title so that visitors can find the main entrance to your site.

The page title is used in three important places when browsing the Web. First, it's displayed at the top of the user's browser window. Secondly, it's used as the title for a bookmark index if a user has created a bookmark to your page. Thirdly, and most importantly, it is used as the title for your index entry for the page, as created by the search engine.

meta-tags
To help the search engine correctly analyse and index your site, you add special codes into the file that's used to store the webpage.

These codes, called meta-tags, are an extension to the HTML language (used to lay the page out) and are only used for indexing – they're not displayed.

The meta-tags need to be added manually to each page. Most Web design software lets you add these using a special form; if not, you will have to edit the text file that contains the webpage, using Windows Notepad or a similar text editor. If you add the tags manually, they need to be in the first few lines of the file, in the <HEADER> . . . </HEADER> section.

First, type in the key words for the page (normally between 10 and 50 words) that someone might type in at a search engine to find your site. These are used by the search engine to index the page directly. For example, if you sell telephone equipment, you could use words such as 'telephone, exchange, PABX, wireless, communications, telecom' and so on. This entry would look like this:

```
<META NAME=''KEYWORDS'' CONTENT=''telephone,
exchange, PABX, wireless, communications, telecom''>
```

Next, you need to write a concise description of what's on the page. Don't write more than 30–40 words and make sure you include a clear description within the first few words. This description is often displayed by the search engine if it matches a search by a user. If you don't include this description, the engine will use the first chunk of text it finds on the page. Here's an example for our fictitious telephone supplier:

```
<META NAME=''DESCRIPTION'' CONTENT=''Telephone
equipment exchanges and PABX devices installed quickly
and efficiently for your office telecommunications with
great prices on the latest ISDN-based integrated
telephone systems''>
```

submit your site to search engines

Once you have prepared each page in your website with a title and the two different meta-tags, you are ready to submit the pages to the search engines. As mentioned earlier, you can do this manually by visiting each of the major search engines and manually completing a submission form, or you can use a commercial service that will automatically submit your information to a range of sites. If you are in a hurry, use one of the automatic submission services such as SubmitIt! (www.submit-it.com), Exploit (www.exploit.com), did-it (www.did-it.com) or All4One (www.all4one.com), or use the tools provided by business portals such as Microsoft's bCentral (www.bcentral.com). However, since each search engine has slightly different registration requirements, you will get a better fit if you have the time to visit each manually.

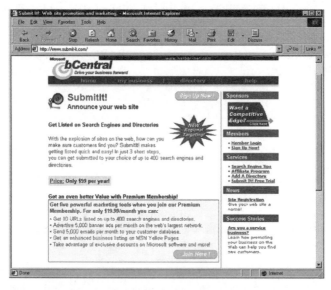

Figure 5.2 Automatic tools like SubmitIt! register your new site's details with hundreds of search engines

As well as being different, the submission requirements for search engines tend to change. The most important is a good submission to Yahoo!. Visit its submission instruction page (www.yahoo.com/docs/info) to make sure that you follow the instructions carefully. You can keep up to date with current information about submission methods by looking at the invaluable www.searchenginewatch.com website.

If you only have time to register with a few search engines, make sure that you cover the following sites with a personal visit and a manual registration – these are the most important search sites on the Web and will benefit from this tailored approach. The other search sites can be covered using an automated submission service.

- www.altavista.com
- www.excite.com
- www.hotbot.com
- www.infoseek.com
- www.lycos.com
- www.yahoo.com
- www.webcrawler.com

You'll find a special link on the first page of each of these sites that takes you to the submission form. The best approach is to look at a submission form – even print it out – then spend some time offline looking at the sections of the form and writing on your word-processor suitable text for each section (such as short description, long description, category etc.). When you have polished these texts, go online again, revisit the search sites and simply copy and paste your main text into the fields, editing as required to suit the different search engines.

Generally, your site will be added to the index after a few days, a week at most. If you want to submit your site to a country-specific search engine, such as Yahoo UK (www.yahoo.co.uk), you can duplicate the effort and enter the information on the main US site (www.yahoo.com).

online review and what's new listings

Most Internet users like to keep up to date with what's new on the Web and will often visit a new site if it's been reviewed, mentioned in a magazine or given an interesting write-up. This can be enough to spread the word that your site is worth a look. There are dozens of 'what's new' sites that have evolved into very popular websites in their own right. In addition, most newspapers, business and technology magazines carry features on the latest interesting websites. And a surefire way to increase traffic is to win an award from a magazine or other review panel (awards are handed out frequently, but still prove that a site is worth a visit).

Figure 5.3 Internet magazines often include sections for new or the best sites

The review, what's new and awards sites vary greatly: some are a simple listing, others a comprehensive editorial review from a panel of experts. Some charge, but most are a free service and it's worth submitting your new site to each. And if the review panel think your site is good enough, you could even get an award that will help attract visitors.

The directories are run by a range of organisations, from Internet magazines – these tend to display a small number of sites that have been reviewed – to large search engines, companies or hobbyists. With the exception of the major 'new' directory sites (listed below), the other directories tend to come and go. Turn the tables and use a search engine to find the latest sites that contain a 'what's new' section.

- www.yahoo.com/picks
- www.netscape.com
- www.internet-magazine.com
- www.netmag.co.uk
- www.iwks.com
- www.go.com
- www.ask.com
- www.about.com

Visit AwardSites (www.awardsites.com) for its list of over 600 award and 'what's new' sites.

reciprocal links

A good way of reaching a niche market is to research (see Chapter 11) the other websites that cover the same subject and ask if they will carry a link to your website. Make it a reciprocal deal and offer to include a link back to their site. With the exception of direct competitors, most other related sites should be happy to include a reciprocal link; they too are trying to promote their site. For example, if you restore old Maserati cars, you could ask for reciprocal links with the various Maserati club websites. Some of the first places to ask about a reciprocal link are:

- **Trade organisations** – almost every industry has at least one related trade organisation; they might have a list of member companies or related links that could prove to be a good source of visitors to your site.
- **Related businesses** – your business will have close ties to dozens of other companies including your distributors, customers or partners.

■ **Similar profile sites** – find sites that might attract a similar user profile.

■ **Analysis of log files** – look carefully at your access log files to see which are the popular referrer sites (the sites that are visited just before a surfer comes to your site); visit these sites and see if they would be complementary to your company's marketing profile.

■ **BusinessLink and local government sites** – local government schemes, such as BusinessLink (www.businesslink.co.uk), include resource pages with links to local suppliers and specialists.

promote your website

Make sure that you take every opportunity to remind your potential customers that you have a website. Once your site is up and running, and indexed by all the major search engines, you should be easy to find. When you create advertisements, include your domain name and an e-mail contact on each advert. Similarly, make sure that new catalogues, price lists and flyers all have your website address. Conventions usually print a catalogue of exhibitors and are often used as a reference by visitors – make sure that your catalogue entry includes your website address.

Don't forget to add your website address to your e-mail and newsgroup signature file – the text that's added to the end of all e-mail messages or newsgroup postings you send. All e-mail software lets you create a signature (for example in Microsoft Internet Explorer, choose Tools/Options/Signatures) that should be just a few lines long and include your name, company, motto and website address. When you send e-mail, the signature reinforces the company brand. When you post a message to a newsgroup, discussion group or mailing list, the signature file is effectively your company's only advertising.

To help spread the message that you have a new website, consider these promotional ideas, all covered in detail elsewhere in this book:

■ Banner advertising (see Chapter 6).
■ Press releases (see Chapter 10).

▨ Announce the site to customers and remind them with news-letters (see Chapter 4).
▨ Target new and existing customers with a direct e-mail campaign (see Chapter 8)
▨ Carefully monitor and contribute to newsgroups, discussion groups and mailing lists (see Chapter 8).

advertising on the Web

Almost every major website features advertising: the long, thin banner ads tempting users to click and be transported to another site. In theory, the Internet advertising model seems near perfect: using visitor analysis (see Chapter 7) you can target your ads so that they are displayed to a niche range of viewers, selected by country of origin or subject of interest, the production costs are low, advertising costs are similar to print media, and you can very accurately measure response.

Some of the most sophisticated advertising sites are the large, popular search engines (such as About, Excite and Yahoo!). These search sites have an added bonus for advertisers – a particular advert can be displayed in response to the keyword a visitor uses in a search. If a visitor searches for plumbing suppliers, they'll get the results of the search plus banner ads from your plumbing supply company.

Online advertising provides an exciting new market and outlet: it complements traditional advertising media and can reach niche targets very effectively. To cover the new technology, there is a new language to describe the medium, a different way of pricing and specialist online ad agencies who can buy or sell advertising space.

Advertising on the Web has become another way of promoting a product or service, complementing traditional media such as print, TV, radio and direct mail. Most Web-based advertising is in the form of display-style banner ads. The banner image is normally hyperlinked to another site – if a viewer clicks on the banner, they'll jump to the advertiser's site.

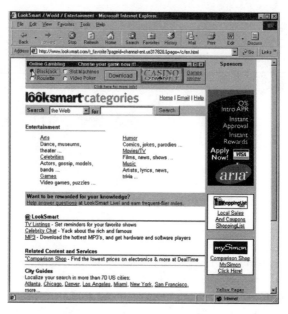

Figure 6.1 Most popular free sites, such as LookSmart, now fit banner ads around the content

Banner ads have settled into two main standard sizes: 468 × 60 or (sometimes) 100 × 75 pixels. The image for the advert is normally stored as a GIF or JPEG format image file and created using a standard image or paint program. Within the banner's space, you can design almost anything and include a photograph, text, drawings or animation. See the Directory, page 152, for details of sites that can help you design and place your banner advert.

Web vs print media

Web advertising sounds great in theory, but how does it compare to print adverts in a magazine? There are plenty of sceptics who explain often painfully obvious lessons; advertising in a high-profile magazine is expensive, but media-buying agencies who support print media have worked out a range of interesting, and often Web-bashing, figures.

If you buy a four-colour, full-page advert in a magazine, it will usually cost you between $20 and $40 on a CPM basis (cost per thousand, using the number of readers and subscribers). Assuming that only two-thirds of these readers will actually see your advert, this increases the cost to between $30 and $60 CPM. This figure compares poorly with Web-based advertising, which charges from $20 CPM (although many specialist sites charge several times this rate). However, this is a passive view rate, not a click-through CPA rate, which is often just a percent or two of the total viewers.

Would you rather pay for a small banner ad in a relatively new market or, for a little more, get a large, full-colour ad in a high-profile magazine? If you're promoting a website, the Web-based solution makes sense. If you're selling a product, using the Web as a new channel, you might find that print ads work better for your type of product.

the cost of advertising

If you want to display your banner advertisement on a commercial site, you will probably be charged for it (although there are free banner exchange cooperatives, see later in this chapter). There is a range of different schemes used to charge for essentially the same service, but most sites provide a price chart (or rate card) based on two schemes, according to the number of people that see your advert or the number of people that click on your advert.

There are two important terms to remember when comparing the costs of advertising: 'impression' and 'click-through'. When a banner advertisement on a webpage is shown to a user, this is called an impression. When a banner advertisement is displayed on a webpage and a user clicks on it and is then transferred to another website, this is called a click-through. Most sites will charge you per impression, often termed CPM (cost per thousand impressions) or CPI (cost per impression). Paying by impression is fine if you want to display your message, but if you want to pay by results, try and get a click-through advertising rate, often termed CPA (cost per action). The far simpler alternative is to pay a day rate, where your advert is displayed on a per-day basis; this is often used in directories that support advertorial (text written by you about your products).

Most websites that accept banner ads have a range of charges for banner ads, depending where on their site you want the ad displayed. CPM rates – the cost of displaying your banner advert – normally range anywhere from $20 to $200 per thousand times your ad is displayed. CPA rates – paying per click-through – are often far, far higher and generally much harder to agree on.

conversion rates

The most important factor in assessing how effective advertising will be for you is the conversion rate of visitors versus impressions – that is, how many people will take notice of your banner ad and click on it? This click-through rate (CTR) is expressed as a percentage. At the start of the Web revolution the CTR of a banner ad was about 2 per cent: for every 1000 times your banner image was displayed, 20 viewers clicked on it to find out more. Unfortunately, surfers have become bored with ads and current average CTR numbers have shrunk to just 1 per cent. Some tricks help – if your banner artwork uses snazzy animated graphics you can improve your CTR by 25 per cent, and if you target a very specialist niche user profile your CTR can increase to near 10 per cent.

If you plan on advertising on a big, general-purpose website, such as Yahoo!, you might expect a CTR of around 1 or 2 per cent. However, by restricting your advert to a particular niche area of Yahoo!, you can increase the rate of return – unfortunately, this will also cost more. Some websites can provide targeted placement for you, for example showing your advert in response to a user's search query on a particular key word. If you sell exhaust systems, you could elect to show your ad if users type in 'exhaust' or 'car service'. This improves CTR but, again, is charged at around twice the basic rate.

Figure 6.2 Doubleclick is one of the biggest online ad agencies in the market

The final blow is that, unfortunately for the advertisers, in reality many surfers ignore the ads, many find them intrusive and irritating and, for those who feel strongly on the issue, there is special software that will strip out ads before they are ever displayed. One of the main complaints from users is that ads take time to download and slow down the surfing experience.

To check on current prices, see if the site where you want to advertise has a rate card displayed. Otherwise, look to one of the specialist media agency buying services, who also provide reports on banner ad trends and summaries:

- www.doubleclick.com
- www.engage.com/ipro/
- www.webtrack.com
- www.activemediaresearch.com

free banner advertising

The Internet was built on the principles of free access – and this has even permeated the commercial world of advertising. If you don't have the money to carry out a comprehensive banner ad campaign, you can still get your banner ad displayed on hundreds of other sites using one of the many free banner exchange cooperatives, such as LinkExchange (www.bcentral.com). See the Directory, page 152, for a list of free banner exchange schemes. The catch with all of these schemes is that you have to accept other people's adverts on your site in return for having your ad displayed.

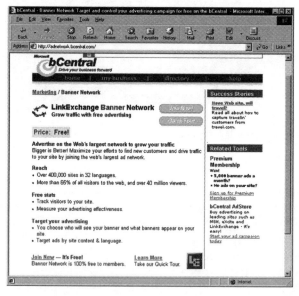

Figure 6.3 You can get free advertising on the LinkExchange cooperative, but in exchange you'll have to display ads

However, LinkExchange is simple to use and does ensure that your ads are seen across a wide range of sites. Once you've registered (for free), you define the subject area of your products and submit your banner artwork. In exchange, you need to add a special line of code in one of your webpages. Each time your webpage is displayed by a visitor, this line of code will automatically pull off a random banner image from the LinkExchange library (in the category that you have chosen) and display it on your site. Your advert is distributed in the same way over the other sites in the scheme.

buying ad space at auction

An alternative way to find cheap advertising space is to bid at an auction of surplus ad space. If a site has surplus capacity or an advertiser pulls out, the excess space might be sold at one of the online auctions. These don't get much for the site hosting the ad-verts – prices can be as low as $1–$5 CPM – but they do give advertisers a chance to place trial ads on sites that they might not otherwise consider. The available ad spaces are listed by the auto-mated auction system and the highest bidder wins. The best-known online auction house is AdBot (www.adbot.com).

designing a banner

Designing a banner advertisement can be a tricky business. You only have a tiny image with which to attract the viewer's attention, tell them about a product or service and tempt them on to your site. If your banner ad is boring, you've effectively wasted your money.

As explained above, there are two main sizes of banner ads, mea-sured in pixels (the smallest unit in an image editing program): ad images are either 468 pixels wide by 60 pixels high or sometimes 100 pixels wide by 75 pixels high. Generally, there's also a maximum file size associated with any ad image of 7Kb. Most ad images are stored in the GIF image file format, which also lets you incorporate anima-tion and special effects – all of which take up more space (hence the maximum limit on the file size).

When you create your banner image, check carefully with the site where you plan to display the ad on the formats and sizes for the image. Most sites expect the image to be in a GIF file format, but

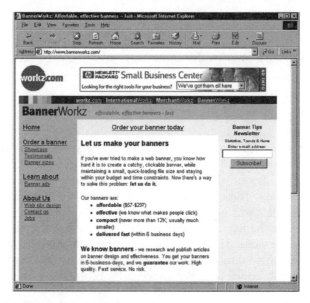

Figure 6.4   Specialist sites help produce an effective banner ad design

some prefer the JPEG file format (this has better colour support and provides better quality for photos than GIF).

You can design your banner advert yourself, using almost any image editor that supports the GIF or JPEG file formats – for example, the popular Paintshop Pro (www.jasc.com) provides image painting and editing tools. Alternatively, you could use a specialist banner ad designer – see the Directory, page 152, for a range of sites that offer this service.

However you design your banner ad, make sure that you take into account these tips:

■ In print media, the best slot is opposite editorial matter; online, try to ensure that your banner is at the top of the page.

■ Keep the message simple – and use just a few words or a short sentence.

■ Don't bother describing the product in detail, just use a catchy phrase.

■ Try to include a call to action to increase response.

■ Pose a question to gain attention.

- Make sure that the banner is relevant to the viewer.
- Don't over-use one banner design; on a general, high-traffic site, change after 100 000 impressions.
- Make sure that any click-throughs go to a relevant webpage on your site rather than the main home page.
- Use animation to attract attention.
- Don't use lewd or sexist images.
- Try to incorporate your company name and website on the banner.
- A simple trick – adding the words 'click me' improves response!
- Including the word 'free' on the banner always improves response.
- Don't forget to add a descriptive alternative text (using the HTML ALT tag) – over 10 per cent of surfers switch off inline images, so won't see your banner ad artwork.

The final aspect of placing a banner ad is to monitor the response to the advert. Unlike print media, where it can be difficult to identify calls generated from an advert, you can use access log analysis (see Chapter 7) to monitor your visitor trends. If you place a banner ad, try to link it to a particular webpage rather than your main home page, which will give you a good idea of the response to this advert. Using log analysis you can check the profile of visitors attracted by your ad – even by country of origin. Link the advertising and response and make changes to your ad to finetune it to the emerging profile of your visitors.

electronic coupons and tokens

One of the latest, and most popular, alternative advertising techniques on the Web is promoting your site using electronic tokens. You collect points by surfing to various (nominated) sites who give points in exchange for a purchase or simply for visiting. The user can then redeem their points for gifts or products. This works well and helps attract (admittedly price-conscious) visitors to your site –

great if you have a very consumer-oriented mass-market product, but not much use if you're selling executive jets.

There are two major schemes: ipoints (www.ipoints.co.uk) lets you rack up special points as you spend in participating shops, then trade in the points for free books, CDs or flights. Beenz (www.beenz.com) lets you collect points as you visit any of the affiliated sites. You don't have to spend anything, just visit the sites and click on the Beenz button. Once you've enough Beenz currency, you can trade it in for discounts at affiliated sites. It's a clever – and free – marketing tool that's rapidly attracting new affiliates and users.

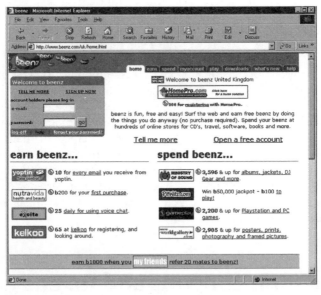

Figure 6.5 Beenz lets visitors collect points as they browse, then exchange these for goods

An alternative idea is to use electronic coupons. The latest electronic version of traditional printed coupons lets you visit a central coupon site, check the area that interests you, download the relevant coupons, print them out and get a rebate or discount.

Two of the most popular coupon distribution sites are Coupons (www.coupon.com) and eCoupons (www.ecoupons.com). You can advertise on both sites within a particular relevant section or you can place your own coupons online to get visitors to try your product with an initial discount offer.

measuring response

An essential part of any marketing effort is the ability to monitor the response to the campaign. On the Net, you can measure who's visiting your website and what they view and do when they are browsing on your site. You can set up a simple counter to measure how many people stop by your site but, for in-depth analysis, you need to use the detailed access logs that record every action of a visitor.

The next, more advanced, stage of visitor response is predictive software that shows them what they would like to see, based on their own information. For example, many of the biggest websites use sophisticated software to trace the actions of a visitor, then display relevant material or adverts related to their actions. If someone on Yahoo! checks the weather in New York, special software at Yahoo! spots this trend and could display banner ads from services in the city.

However, the real benefit of visitor analysis is that it provides the key to effective marketing on the Internet. Unless you are selling a product via the Internet, the only way you can measure the success of your online efforts is in increased numbers of visitors entering your website. In traditional fields of marketing, the only way to judge the response of a campaign is to ask the reader or viewer to respond to an advertisement. With the Internet, you don't need to ask the users or customers questions – your software can automatically find out their country of origin, which of your products they prefer and where else they have been browsing!

And finally, use access log analysis to find out which website the user visited before they came to your site. Contact the most popular referrer – if it's not a competitor – and see if you can add exchange links, or banner adverts, or even create a special discount or offer for your products that's then advertised on their website.

counting visitors

One of the simplest ways of checking the number of visitors is a Web counter. You've probably seen dozens of sites that use this feature: it's a tachometer-style counter at the bottom of the page that displays a message 'you are visitor number 1133'. And for anything other than a hobbyist's site, they look terrible.

The Web counter works via a tiny Perl program that runs on your Web server: the program creates a file, then stores the number one in the file. Each time the home page for the website is accessed, the program runs, reads the current number in the file and increments this. You can then display the number stored in the file to see how many people have visited your page. Or, more accurately, how many times that webpage has been viewed.

There are several problems with counters. First, they look terrible. Secondly, they can give the wrong impression – do you really want new visitors to your site to know that they are visitor number 14? Thirdly, they don't give a true impression of who's visiting your site – maybe a visitor has bookmarked another page within your site, in which case the counter would not trigger.

If you really do want to use a counter on your site, here's how to do it: add a line of code to the HTML instructions in a webpage file. For example, if you want to use the free Web counter script provided by the Demon ISP in an imaginary site called 'www.mycompany. co.uk', you would add the following line in your webpage:

```
<IMG SRC=''www.demon.co.uk/cgi-bin/
Counter.cgi?www.mycompany.co.uk.index.html''>
```

All ISPs should provide some sort of counter script or other facility – if they don't, you could use a free service, such as Digits (www.digits.com), but because this is a popular site it can be slow, or try the more comprehensive ShowStat (www.showstat.com).

access logs

Every time a visitor looks at your website, you can record information about them: which country they come from, which products interest them most, how long they stayed, even what type of computer they are using. All this information can be recorded automatically in an access log – a file of visitor activity that's generated automatically by your ISP or Web space provider. The data within the file provides a wealth of information about the people who visit your site, what they look at and how long they stay; the access log is one of your best sources of information to analyse trends and response in your website.

Access logs are created by software running on your Web server computer, hosted by your ISP or Web space provider. This software records details of everything that the Web server has to do in response to a visitor's requests, from displaying a webpage or

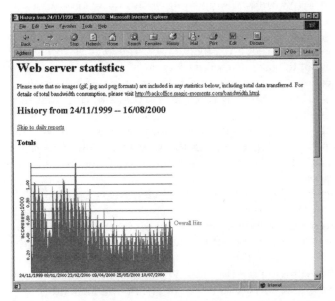

Figure 7.1 A simple graphical access log provides a basic view of your site's popularity

running a search script to ordering information or viewing images. The log software runs automatically and stores its results in an (often very large) access log file. Once you have an access log, you can use specialist software to analyse the information to find out more about the visitors to your site.

The access log records visitor actions in very fine detail. For example, if a user visits your website, they'll start by seeing your home page (normally stored in a file index.html). To view this page, the user's Web browser sends a GET request to the Web server to ask for the page. The Web server sends the HTML file back to the browser and waits for the next request. If your index.html page has any images, these need to be requested separately, again using GET commands. This means that one user's visit to your site can result in a dozen lines in the access log.

Some people mistakenly call each line in an access log a 'hit', which can lead to much confusion when trying to work out how many visitors your site gets. For example, if your home page has three images, one visitor would generate four hits in the access log. If they move somewhere else then decide to return to the home page, the same person generates another four hits.

Each line within the access log has the time, command and file name that was requested by the user. The log also records information about the user, gathered by asking the user's own Web browser a question. For example, most access logs will record the type of browser that the user is running, the domain name that the user is working from and, in some cases, also the name of the last website that the user visited! All this information is stored by the user's browser and, depending on the way the browser works, can be automatically reported if the access log software asks the right questions.

The way in which this raw data in the access log is stored depends on the software running on the Web server – for most users this is a choice made by the ISP or Web space hosting company. However, the most common format for storing logged data follows the Common Log Format (or NCSA) specification. Almost all access log analysis software can read this type of data file and use it to produce meaningful reports on the type of visitor you have on your site.

The data in an access log file is stored automatically, but you will need to ask your ISP to switch on this feature. You will also need to

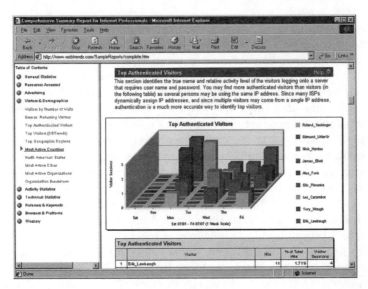

Figure 7.2 Site log analysis helps you identify trends and types of visitor to your site

acquire and install a log analysis software package; there are many types on the market, described in the next few pages.

The access log data is usually stored as plain text which can be viewed or edited with any text editor, though this serves little purpose! By using analysis software, you'll be able to identify key indicators that you can use to tailor your marketing strategy. For example, you can view:

- the country of origin of your visitors
- the products (or webpages) that interest particular visitors
- the success of a special offer or new product
- the source of your visitors – whether from a search engine reference or linked site
- the success of a banner ad
- response to print or e-mail campaigns that specify a particular webpage.

The analysis software can either be run on your own computer or on the Web server where your website is stored. The former is the most common solution, but it does mean that you have to transfer the data to your computer; the latter cuts this stage out, but normally requires you to install and configure an application on your Web server.

The dominant software for desktop-based log analysis is WebTrends (www.webtrends.com); some ISPs supply this software free of charge, but otherwise you can purchase the software online. This particular product plots graphs of visitor activity and generates reports summarising visitor profiles for your site – all essential information when planning and running a marketing campaign. There are several alternative products, mostly shareware editions, that you can try out for free – search Yahoo! (www.yahoo.com) for 'access log' to find the section detailing current developer websites.

The most popular Web server-based applications are written in the Perl programming language and need to be installed on your Web server – it's not difficult, but it can be a time-consuming process and you might need assistance from your ISP. Two of the most popular programs that work in this way include Analog (www.statslab.cam.ac.uk/~sret1/analog) and MKStats (available from many sources, search Yahoo! for your nearest site).

analysing your site visitors

Access log analysis software can produce a mass of different reports, including tables of visitor numbers, hits per page, graphs of visitors per day of the week, and lists of countries of origin. The reports all vary in design and presentation but the underlying data is the same. To understand how the graphs and tables are produced, you should understand what information is contained in the raw data stored in a log file.

Each line of the file contains a list of data describing the event that occurred. As explained above, if a visitor looks at your home page, they are submitting a request to view the file that contains this webpage (normally stored in a file called 'index.html'). If your home page contains images, each image is normally retrieved in a series of separate operations. Each of these generates a line in the access log. Below are the basic chunks of data that form each entry within a log file.

geographic location

One of the most interesting – and most misleading – reports shows a breakdown of users according to their geographic location. These results are derived from the characters at the right-hand end of the user's domain name. For example, 'microsoft.co.uk' is based in the UK, whereas 'microsoft.co.au' is based in Australia. US-based and international companies tend to prefer the '.com' suffix but this is difficult for analysis tools to assign to a specific country. An anomaly that you'll spot is that all CompuServe and AOL members, regardless of where they live, are noted as resident of Virginia, USA. A small town will seem to make up a vast proportion of your visitors!

domain name

This second report uses the same data as the geographic location report. However, the analysis tool totals the number of hits from each domain or host name. This gives a good idea of your customer base and can help solve problems thrown up by the geographic location report – for example, a large percentage of users who are registered with CompuServe.

Another way of using this report is to check if your competitors have been looking at your website, for how long and at which particular products or sections. Alternatively, see if there are any companies or educational institutions (both types of organisation normally have their own unique domain names) that have made considerable use of your site. Again, if it is an educational domain name (with .edu or .ac in the name), then perhaps your site appears as a reference in a course or a librarian is interested in your product or someone is interested in evaluating your products.

page requests

One of the most useful reports you can get from log analysis software details the popularity of the different webpages on your website. This can give you a clear impression of which product or service – or feature of your site – is working and how best to allocate your marketing budget, or even how to develop new product ranges. If you find that some pages are very popular, it's worth adding a direct link to these pages from your main index page. It's good design to allow a user to reach their destination webpage in just three clicks.

browser type

Almost all access logs record the make and brand of Web browser that your visitor is running – this is recorded automatically and, although it seems an odd piece of data to store, it is useful when designing your website. With this piece of information, you can see if the majority of your visitors are using the latest Web browser technology – and so would appreciate JavaScript tricks and the latest multimedia gizmos – or if they are still using an older Web browser and so wouldn't see any of these special effects.

referring domains

The final report of particular interest is one that describes the refer-ring domains – this is the domain (or website) that your visitor browsed immediately before turning to your site. Not all Web browsers give out this information to a Web access log, but if they do, it can offer interesting data that can help build a profile of your visitors and provide new marketing opportunities. For example, if you discover that the majority of your visitors were at the search engine Yahoo.com, whereas only a few per cent arrived from the Excite.com search engine, you will know that you should concen-trate on improving your index entry at Excite and perhaps advertis-ing at Yahoo!.

This is also a good way of spotting potential partners and com-petitors. For example, if you see that a number of visitors come from a competitor's site, you should try to see why they visited your competitor before you – this could be down to better site marketing or good use of meta-tags (see Chapter 5) or a promo-tional offer.

Lastly, you can use the referring domains report to check if your site could work more closely with another company. If you discover that visitors looking for your range of exhaust systems all visited a particular garage site before your website, it may suggest that the garage has a link to your site and you might consider closer cooperation or a banner advert exchange.

direct
marketing

Direct marketing is a great way to reach an audience. Traditionally, direct marketing uses the postal service; on the Internet, companies use electronic mail to send updates, offers, messages and newsletters to existing and potential customers quickly, efficiently and very cheaply. E-mail is an efficient way to keep in touch with customers and streamline the way you:

- keep existing customers up to date with news and promotions
- gain new customers by sending a cold-call mail shot to a targeted list
- keep distributors and sales reps up to date with offers, prices and new products
- keep in touch with journalists and send out press releases.

E-mail provides a near-perfect medium for direct marketing: every user has a unique e-mail address and their e-mail messages generally appear directly on their desktop; with the traditional postal service, your mail shot has to get through the postroom and past the secretary before it hits the target's desk. E-mail is also very cheap, with near zero delivery costs. Unfortunately, just about every Net-aware company has started using e-mail to target customers and, as a result, users are getting overwhelmed with often unwanted junk mail.

To send a direct marketing piece by e-mail you need a list of the customers' e-mail addresses. You can gather the addresses yourself by asking existing customers to send you their address, or rent a list from a specialist broker. If you use any bought-in list, make sure that the contacts on the list are 'opt-in' users (see below) and that the broker is a member of a known direct mail trade organisation.

At the start of its development, the Internet banned almost all business and commercial traffic – e-mail was merely a good way for colleagues in academia to keep in touch. When the ban on commercial traffic was lifted in the mid-1990s, the direct e-mail concept became tarnished almost immediately. Over-eager (and thoughtless) companies sent out unsolicited advertising messages to millions of random, unknown users. In every case, the plan backfired and simply generated a lot of flame (hate mail) messages.

Follow the simple rules and you won't suffer from any backlash by the recipients. If you ignore these rules and send a message to a million unknown users, you'll get a stack of rude messages in return and will probably be thrown off the Net by your ISP.

getting a list of addresses

The best way to get a list of people interested in receiving news about your products is to ask them. If you send out printed catalogues, advertise your e-mail update service with an e-mail address for new subscribers. Also, add a simple form to your website and encourage visitors to type in their e-mail address to receive regular updates, newsletters or special offers. In both cases, make sure to include reference to a webpage that details your company's privacy policy with regard to the e-mail addresses. If you plan to re-sell the addresses, say so. If you don't (and visitors would much prefer it if you didn't), make this policy clear. Visit the US-based Direct Marketing Association for its guidelines on privacy (www.the-dma.org).

Unsolicited mail shots have a justifiably terrible reputation; if you want to keep a good reputation on the Net, don't use them. An unsolicited mail shot involves sending out thousands (often hundreds of thousands) of messages to unknown people using a rented address list. Since it's unlikely that the recipients asked to receive messages, they will probably delete any junk mail immediately. Some will reply with a rude message (a flame message) and some

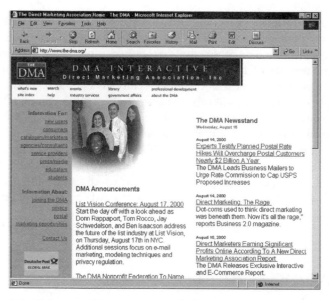

Figure 8.1 Before sending out an e-mail shot, make sure you're following the good advice from the DMA

will contact their ISP to complain. In turn, your ISP will probably close down your Internet account. There are lots of companies who offer to supply a database file with millions of e-mail addresses for next to nothing, but if you use one you're guaranteed to ruin your company's reputation.

A step away from an unsolicited mail shot is a semi-researched campaign. Instead of renting a list with a million addresses, you do your own research and pull addresses from parts of the Internet that cater to a related subject. For example, if you plan to market a new tennis racket cover, you could visit newsgroups covering tennis and start to record e-mail addresses of people who post messages. In theory this is a reasonable idea, however most newsgroup users are wise to this – first, they hate receiving messages in this way, and secondly, they often use a false e-mail address to prevent this happening.

The best route for direct e-mail marketing is to use an opt-in mailing list. This is a list of e-mail addresses of users who have specifically said that they are willing to receive advertising messages about a particular type of product. Typically, these are collected from big consumer sites that ask users to register before offering a free service such as an e-mail address or Web space. Most of the reputable companies that rent out mailing lists will offer opt-in lists; use one of these well-known brokers to find a suitable list, ask your local direct marketing association for a list of registered E-list brokers, or visit the excellent EverythingEmail (www. everythingemail.com), which provides a good place to start. Alternatively, try one of these brokers:

- Copywriter   www.copywriter.com/lists
- InBox Express   www.inboxexpress.com
- PostMasterDirect   www.postmasterdirect.com
- Targ-it   www.targ-it.com

sending e-mail

Once you have your e-mail address list, you need to consider how to send the mail shot. Some e-mail software provides features to support mailing lists with hundreds of entries, but for thousands or tens of thousands of addresses, you need to use different techniques.

For small lists of addresses, it's probably more convenient to use your normal e-mail software. Pegasus, Outlook and Netscape Mail all support multiple address books that let you mail-merge a message with a list of addresses. Similarly, most high-end contact-management software (such as ACT!, GoldMine or Maximizer) also supports this mail-merge feature.

For mail shots with thousands of addresses, you might find that your e-mail software will not work (Outlook Express, for example, limits distribution lists to around 100 entries). One alternative is to link a database with your e-mail software; Microsoft Access can feed addresses to Microsoft Outlook, creating a mail package that supports hundreds of thousands of addresses. Alternatively, use specialist mail software such as Campaign (www.arialsoftware.com) that provides dedicated mail management software. For a list of specialist software, look to the EverythingEmail (www.everything email.com) resource site that lists software manufacturers.

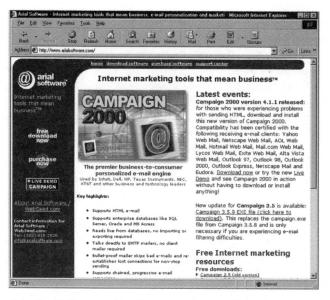

Figure 8.2 Specialist e-mail software makes sending thousands of messages easier

The problem with both these systems is that they send messages via your ISP and standard Internet connection. That is not an issue for 100 or so messages, but the process could take hours if you want to send thousands of messages, tying up your computer and connection. Worse, your ISP might block this type of transfer, even if you are using an opt-in list. The solution for large lists, particularly newsletters or bulletins, with tens of thousands of addresses, is to use software that runs on an Internet server rather than on your desktop computer. These software products (normally called majordomo, list server or mail server) run on a server computer linked to the Net – typically where you have your Web space or your ISP. The software is a relatively simple script that takes a message stored in a file and automatically sends it to a list of users whose addresses are stored in another file. Just one command starts the process and frees up your desktop and connection to the Net.

There are dozens of different majordomo products available, mostly shareware or freeware. One of the most popular is Majordomo (www.majordomo.com), or you could search the software

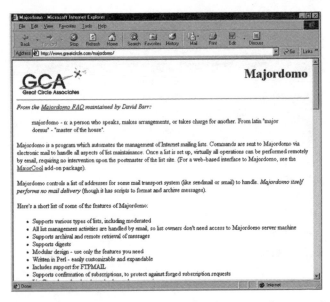

Figure 8.3   To help manage and run a mailing list, use software such as the popular Majordomo

libraries such as FreeCode (www.freecode.com) and ScriptSearch (www.scriptsearch.com). Installing the software can be difficult, so ask your ISP or Web space hosting company to help you set it up. If your ISP does not want you to install this type of software or thinks that you will use it to send out millions of unwanted spam messages, turn to a company to manage the list for you, such as SparkLIST (www.sparklist.com), or use a free service such as ListBot (www.listbot.com) – though the free services tend to add a line of their own advertising at the bottom of each message.

the message

The final piece in the direct mail puzzle is the mailing itself. There are different types of message you can send and different ways to format the content. Unlike a traditional printed mailing item, your design and creative efforts will be limited by the technology available.

A single cold-call e-mail message can be useful, but a better long-term solution is to start a regular newsletter-style bulletin. Some e-mail newsletters provide a regular update about a niche field – for example the topic-specific marketing newsletter from Wilson Internet (www.wilsonweb.com) – or can be company specific about your range of products, special offers and updates.

how often?

Start on a modest scale. Producing a regular newsletter takes a lot of time and effort; a one-off is easy, but if you promise the subscribers detailed information every week, you will need to set aside time or get a writer or editor on your team. If you are producing a company-specific newsletter, start with a two-monthly general update newsletter then, if there's sufficient demand, change this to a monthly schedule.

design and format

Many e-mail newsletters are now available in two formats. The first is a plain text message that can be read with just about any type of e-mail software, from a PC to a WAP phone. The second is a highly formatted message that includes images, animation, colour and formatted text. The latter is great if your users have the latest e-mail software (such as Microsoft Outlook) that can display these formatted messages; anyone with older software will see nothing.

If your newsletter content would benefit from images and formatting, create two separate lists: start subscribers with a default setting of the plain text version, but tell them about the more elaborate, formatted edition and give its e-mail address. Companies such as the daily news service InfoBeat (www.infobeat.com) and auction site Lastminute (www.lastminute.com) both offer two types of e-mail newsletter – plain and simple or highly formatted.

To create your newsletter, use a standard wordprocessor or your e-mail software's editor. If you're using a wordprocessor, don't forget to turn off the special formatting features (such as curly quote

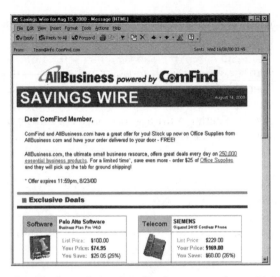

Figure 8.4 ComFind.com keeps its subcribers up to date with highly
formatted, graphical e-mails

marks or automatic copyright symbols) that will not display correctly when viewed with older e-mail software.

Formatted e-mail messages are created using HTML, the same
codes used to create a webpage. To construct your formatted newsletter, use a standard webpage design product (see the Directory,
page 147 or your wordprocessor – if it supports HTML. Each e-mail
product uses a different system to import formatted messages, so
check how yours works. For example, to send a highly formatted
e-mail message in Microsoft Outlook you have to import your formatted message as a message template, then use this template to
create a new message.

Lastly, send the newsletter to a colleague or back to your own
e-mail address as a test to check that it looks as expected – before
sending it out to your thousands of subscribers.

the content

When writing your newsletter or bulletin, readers will appreciate it
if you follow a similar structure to other newsletters. It makes the

most of their (often very limited) attention span and the medium itself.

- Make your newsletter text short, punchy and – if possible – lively. Keep the dry style for the company report tucked away on your website.
- Start each newsletter with a short contents summary that describes what is in the different parts of the newsletter – this will be the text the reader sees when scanning their new mail.
- Write short articles or summaries of new stories. If you want to provide lots more detail or images, include a hyperlink to more further information on a webpage on your website.
- Try to include something new and useful in each newsletter, rather than just news about your company or products: for example, a tip or how-to or special offer.
- If you reference historical text or articles, include a hyperlink to the relevant text on your website.
- Finish each message with an e-mail contact in case of questions and clear instructions that explain how the subscriber can stop receiving the newsletter.

marketing to newsgroups and mailing lists

Direct marketing to customers via e-mail is a good way to use the Internet to provide a fast, efficient delivery mechanism. However, there are two other sectors of the Internet that offer interesting, if limited, direct marketing potential: mailing lists and newsgroups. Both provide a forum for discussion – with mailing groups you have to subscribe; newsgroups let you dip in at any time to read what's being discussed. Neither forum particularly appreciates blatant marketing efforts, but with care you can help promote your company (or products) and provide useful information to the members of the discussion group.

Discussion groups and mailing lists are a popular and efficient way of distributing information to a group of people (see Chapter 12 for information on subscribing yourself). Everything is done using e-mail messages; a central server keeps a list of subscriber e-mail addresses and simply redistributes messages to all the members in the list. If you want to ask a question or post a reply, it's addressed to the server, which in turn sends this on to all the members in the list. You can keep up with your colleagues or with a discussion about a specialist subject via your e-mail software – simple and effective.

Mailing lists were started by academics but now they cover just about every subject conceivable. There are tens of thousands of mailing lists running, covering everything from classic cars to investment.

Newsgroups work in a different way but provide one of the most active areas of the Internet. A newsgroup is rather like a noticeboard in your office – it's an open forum that allows anyone to post a message and discuss almost anything. There are tens of thousands of individual newsgroups, each providing a discussion forum for a particular subject. To read and post messages to a newsgroup, you need to use special newsreader software (which is usually part of your e-mail program).

Flip to Chapter 12 for information about how to find discussion groups and how to use and subscribe to mailing lists and news-groups that cover your area of interest.

careful marketing

Newsgroups, mailing lists and discussion groups would seem to be an ideal forum to announce a new product or provide information about an upgrade or special offer. If you are launching a new car polish, it appears reasonable to assume that anyone involved in the rec.cars newsgroup or the Maserati mailing list will be interested. Unfortunately for the marketer, almost all newsgroups and mailing lists have a no-business policy. If you post a blatantly commercial message, you'll be flamed (get hate mail) and you will damage your company's reputation.

This is particularly frustrating, since the users fit the perfect customer profile. The best way to tackle these specialist forums is to use a very soft approach to your marketing: monitor the discussions and if someone asks a question or has a problem, answer it sensibly, without any commercial message. Instead, make sure that your signature (the few lines at the bottom of each message) includes your company name and a link to your website. So long as you're contributing something useful to the group, no one will mind. And as a result, some members might even visit your site to see what you do. Do not, under any circumstances, send unsolicited e-mail to someone who has contributed to a newsgroup or mailing list – or buy a list culled from newsgroups. See earlier in this chapter for ways to send targeted e-mail.

nine

E-commerce

Some websites are set up simply as vehicles to trade and make money; other websites trade in order to pay the running costs; the remaining majority of sites are either paid for as part of the marketing budget or run as a hobby by an enthusiast. Often the progression, for company websites, is that they are launched within the marketing budget, then redesigned and relaunched with an E-commerce focus to allow the company's products to be bought online. As described in the first chapter, E-commerce is itself an attraction for many customers and can be used as a marketing tool. For example, if you set up online trading, you get:

- a new shop that's dedicated to your products
- a shop open 24 hours a day that's convenient for overseas customers
- an efficient shop – once set up, it has low running costs and few employee overheads
- an effective 'pull' for your website that provides another reason for people to visit your site
- a way to improve service to existing customers
- an efficient method of testing special offers or checking feedback from advertisements
- a way of extending distribution to countries and areas not otherwise covered
- a way of tracking the buying habits of customers to improve your customer profile.

E-commerce usually refers to an online shop where customers can order, and normally pay for, products or services via the website. The customers need not be consumers, but could be other businesses – for example inter-company sales or distributor-to-company sales can often be streamlined with a dedicated online ordering facility. In addition to this, E-commerce also refers to other ways of making money on the Internet. The best example is selling advertising space on your website.

Figure 9.1 WH Smith's E-commerce site lets you buy books, videos and CDs, but also provides a free reference centre

This chapter provides an overview of all these facets of E-commerce. For a complete guide to this subject, including practical advice on setting up and running your own Web-based shop, see this book's companion volume, *E-Commerce* (ISBN 0-471-49898-X).

your online shop

To create a shop on the Internet you really need to provide visitors with two familiar features: a way for them to select products they want to buy from your catalogue, and a way for them to pay for the products. Both these features are usually provided with a combination of specialist products. Shopping cart software is used to mimic the action browsing in a real shop – new visitors carry their own virtual shopping basket that they can fill with products from your catalogue. At the checkout section, you need to provide special security features to allow a customer to enter their credit card details safely and without threat from hackers. This secure payment webpage also needs a link to a bank that can accept and confirm the credit card details quickly and accurately.

Creating an online shop can be very quick and straightforward, if you accept certain limitations. However, if you want to create a customised shop that looks and works in exactly the way you want, you will probably need expert help. Shopping cart software can be complex to install, and you will need time and patience to learn how the software has to be configured. The alternative is to ask a specialist Web company to create an online shop for you – almost all Web design companies provide this service. Read the section on using Web design companies on page 25. You'll find a comprehensive list of design companies on the Internet Works site (www.iwks.com).

shopping carts

There are several dozen different shopping cart products available: some cost several thousand pounds to buy, others are free, some are limited in their features, some require an expert programmer to configure and install, some can support a thousand product lines, others support five or ten products. If you choose the wrong type of software you will probably end up with an online shop design that doesn't suit you, your customer or your product range.

Shopping cart software can, broadly, be split into two main categories. With the first, turnkey shopping carts, everything is done online: visit a specialist website offering this service and use its set of templates that let you quickly design and set up your own shop by answering a set of questions. The software generates the shop for you, based on your information and, within minutes, you have a working shop. In the second option, custom shopping carts, buy a software package that can then be configured and customised to suit your needs. The software needs to be installed on your Web server (or your Web space provider's server) and is often in the form of Perl scripts or Java code. The first option is simple to configure and has low start-up costs; the second option is generally very flexible, far more complex to configure and install, but often has far lower running costs.

For details and websites of the main shopping cart packages available, see the Directory, page 153.

turnkey shopping carts

This is a simple approach that lets you create an online shop from a pre-configured template. Offered by specialist websites such as Virgin VirginBiz (www.virginbiz.net), Yahoo! Store (www.store. yahoo.com), Demon Commerce (www.demon.net), iCat (www.icat. com), Amazon zShops (www.amazon.com) or Excite Shopping (shopping.excite.com). This generally costs between £30 and £200 per month, depending on the number of products lines you add to

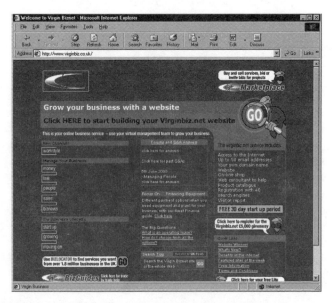

Figure 9.2 Turnkey systems such as VirginBiz can get you up and running quickly, but are not as flexible as a custom shopping cart

your online shop. This fee normally includes credit card processing charges, website hosting, secure payment area and so on.

custom shopping carts

If you are planning an extensive, feature-packed shop, you might find the turnkey shopping cart solution is limiting in its design and range of features. The alternative is to buy or use a free custom shopping cart software program that is installed on your Web server (or your Web space provider's server where you store your website files). Normally, this solution is a trade-off between time and price. If you choose an expensive product, it's often easy to configure and install. The free products can take an expert programmer days or weeks to install. However, they are free! The commercial products, such as COWS (www.cows.co.uk) and Catalog (www.actinic.co.uk), are available from specialist dealers or direct from their developer's website. You'll find dozens of free programs in libraries such as ScriptSearch (www.scriptsearch.com).

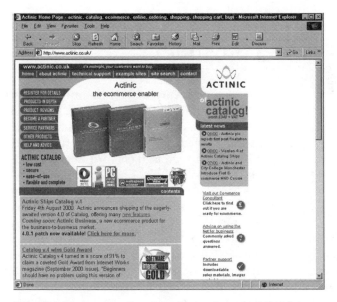

Figure 9.3   Catalog is a popular shopping cart product that lets you set up your own shop

Installing the shopping cart software (especially free products) can be difficult, complex and frustrating – even if you are an expert Perl programmer. To simplify the job, talk to your ISP or Web design company. Almost all business-oriented Web-related companies provide expertise in a particular shopping cart product.

shopping malls

In the early days of the Web, online shopping malls were popular. With this concept, one website provided the base for dozens of online shops selling a range of products, each with a similar look and feel. For example, the best-known UK shopping mall is the pioneering BarclaySquare (www.barclaysquare.co.uk) that includes outlets from NME music shop to The Book People. The mall company helps design and set up your online shop, which then forms part of their mall. You pay a monthly fee or, occasionally, a percentage fee of all sales you complete from the shop. As in a real-life mall, you don't get your own stand-alone site, but you do benefit from the passing trade visiting the mall.

accepting payment

The most commonly accepted currency on the Internet is still the credit card. Almost every adult Web user has one; it's convenient, flexible and relatively safe. In order to accept credit card payments you need to build a section of your Web shop that offers customers a secure place where they can type in their card details and be confident that a hacker can't access these. This is normally carried out using an SSL secure link that encrypts any information transferred between the customer's computer and the server (where the shopping cart is running). Once the shopping cart software has the credit card details, it automatically sends these to a card-authorisation server for approval. Within a couple of seconds, the authorisation computer will either accept or decline the card. The shopping cart can then either confirm the order or ask for another card.

To carry out these steps, you need to set up an account with a card-authorisation company. It in turn will normally require you to

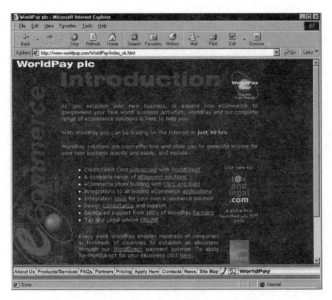

Figure 9.4   WorldPay provides a multi-currency back-end payment system for shops

have a special Internet merchant account with your bank (not the same as a standard credit card merchant account). Finally, your shopping cart software needs to be configured to talk to the authorising company's software.

For details and websites of the main credit card-authorisation companies available, see the Directory, page 154.

costs

When setting up an Internet shop, there are four costs that need to be considered. These are the set-up costs, the running costs, the processing costs and the distribution costs. Some will be paid as fees, sometimes in advance, others are a percentage of the sale, paid when the sale is completed.

The set-up costs normally include buying the shopping cart software, paying your Internet hosting provider for security features such as SSL and perhaps the costs of a designer or programmer. The running costs will include monthly rental for the Web space and security features; if you have decided on a turnkey shopping cart, you'll also have to pay a monthly rental for its services. In addition, you will have to pay a monthly or yearly service charge to the credit card-authorisation company. And lastly, your running costs will include a site manager and customer service staff.

The processing costs are incurred when someone buys something from your shop. The credit card-authorisation service normally charges a percentage fee for each transaction (normally between 1 and 4 per cent). Your bank will also charge you for use of the Internet merchant account (another 1–4 per cent). And your distribution and fulfilment company or warehouse might also charge between 6 and 15 per cent for their work in picking the items, packing and sending off the order.

selling advertising on your site

Selling advertising space on your website is a popular – and potentially lucrative – way of raising money to support your website, content development and running costs. If you are running a heavily branded corporate website, it's unlikely that you will want to sell ad space (and so dilute your message). However, if you have a subject or topic-centred website, then you could find that this appeals to companies trying to reach your particular kind of visitor.

For example, if you manufacture car accessories, your main website might be your corporate catalogue with an online shop and information about your range of spark plugs, car polish and so on. To appeal to a broader audience, you could set up a specialist car website that is not branded with your company's logo but instead promotes discussion and information about car accessories in general. To extend the car metaphor one step further, the specialist Maserati car parts specialist MIE (www.maseratinet.com) in the US has a corporate site that provides an online shop for spare parts and manuals. It also has a separate club site that is designed as a meeting place for enthusiasts and carries discreet information about the other, commercial site.

To appeal to a potential advertiser, your site needs to offer a well-defined, generally niche, audience profile – and regular visitor analysis showing visitor numbers. The potential advertiser will want to see a standard rate card, priced in CPM units (cost per thousand impressions), together with access to audited historical visitor numbers and proof of auditing, reporting and control features for the display of its banner ad. All of these features can be added to your website without undue effort, often using free scripts and software available from software libraries such as ScriptSearch (www.scriptsearch.com) or provided by your Web space host company.

To gauge the viability of your website, here's an example business model. Your website has 30 000 individual visitors (not hits) to your site each month. It targets a niche audience, not a general audience, so your rates might reflect this with slightly higher charges.

Selling five ad slots, each at a modest \$40 CPM, equals $40 \times 30 \times 5$, or \$6000 per month potential income from the five banner ads, assuming that your average 30 000 impressions visit each of the five ads. You would need to analyse your visitor profiles to see how many pages each visitor does view and adjust this figure down accordingly. If you also provide a classified ad section and perhaps a discussion forum, you could charge a slightly higher \$45 CPM for these parts of the site, so generating $45 \times 30 \times 2$, or \$2700 per month. If each visitor sees every ad each time they visit, you would generate a potential annual income of \$104 400.

Unfortunately, your website needs to be very special to attract high-spending companies willing to take out a banner ad. You also need to maintain the software that audits and displays the ads (often called ad farming) and you will probably have to give discounts to the ad agencies that buy ad space for the biggest advertisers.

If you consider your website to be able to provide a good platform for a potential advertiser, but don't want the bother of pitching for ad space and managing the software and auditing process, you might prefer to use a specialist media agency to sell your ad space for you. There are a number of media agencies that buy and sell – and manage the entire display process – for banner ads on your behalf. Some agencies charge a high commission on sales and also pass on office running costs and expenses (so make sure you know the charges before you sign up). However, most provide a very good service. If you want more information, visit specialist agencies such as:

- DoubleClick — www.doubleclick.com
- Beyond Interactive — (www.gobeyond.com)
- Hook Media — (www.hookmedia.com)

The alternative way of selling your ad space is to try the auction system. You're very unlikely to get full rate card for the space, in fact the rates can be as low as $1–$4 CPM, but it's a way of filling what would otherwise be empty banner ad space.

public and press relations

The Internet provides an efficient, fast and effective way to streamline your public and press relations. Both forms of PR are essential to almost every company, and both can be time consuming and rather tedious for day-to-day operations.

When dealing with the media, the Internet helps improve relations and the reach of your PR effort. Many reporters prefer receiving news and press releases via e-mail and, using specialist agencies, you can send out press releases to a targeted group of interested journalists. In addition, you can provide a journalist's library section on your website that includes press contact details, press releases, cuttings, reviews and case study information – helping a journalist who's researching a story. And if you monitor newsgroups and discussion groups, you can often provide information to help journalists who use these forums to ask for opinions or candidates for reviews. Best of all, without printing and mailing costs, your message gets to the reporter's desk quickly and in a very cost-effective way.

Public relations are just as important and you must provide your customers with good service and keep them informed and up to date with news on your products. You could provide a section of your website that includes a database of common questions and answers so you avoid your customers waiting in a telephone queue to speak to support staff. Alternatively, an online conference or discussion group lets customers compare tips or ask questions via a moderator. And don't forget a webpage packed with hints and tips on using your products.

Again, it's well worth monitoring specialist newsgroups, discussion groups and mailing lists – your customers could be complaining about you or your competitors. However, these forums are often used to ask a question about a product or service; monitor the questions and, if they concern part of your company's expertise, give an answer – but don't promote your products too much, instead using a simple signature pointing to your company website.

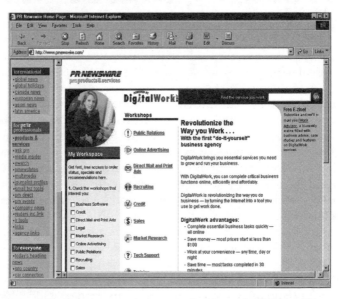

Figure 10.1   Send out press releases via the Net with PR NewsWire

The alternative is to visit a specialist website, such as PR newswire (www.prnewswire.com), one of the main press agency websites that has online request forums allowing reporters to post requests for information, review products and so on.

press relations

Even in this Net-centric age, most of your customers will get information about new products and services from the traditional press, magazines, television and radio. Unlike news-groups, discussion groups or your company website, you can't use new technology directly to influence what appears in these media. You can, however, use the Internet to streamline your distribution of information to the press – with speedy delivery of press releases to a wide range of journalists and maintaining better contact with reporters via e-mail and Net-based discussion forums.

With the exception of straightforward news reporting, journalists (particularly feature writers) use – and often rely on – the Internet as a way of researching their subject. If a journalist is writing a story on a particular product, they can search the Internet to find all the (online) companies that provide this type of product. The companies' websites should provide a complete overview of the products, how they work and how they are marketed. As well as finding a summary of basic features of different brands, the writer can look for technology briefings or background white papers provided by each company to get to know more about research in this niche area. Finally, they can look for research papers on university websites that cover forthcoming developments and go to newsgroups for customer feedback.

press releases

To keep journalists up to date with information about your products, you need to send them a press release for each important event or product launch. Often, these press releases help prompt trade papers and magazines to write about the product launch, event or news. However, with so many press releases being written every day, it's getting harder to ensure that a journalist with an interest in the subject even receives your release. E-mail can help out, with efficient, fast and direct delivery of information to interested journalists. Once you have written your press release, you can send it by e-mail to your existing list of contacts, or you could use a specialist distribution agency to provide worldwide distribution to reporters interested in your subject area.

writing a press release

Writing a press release destined for distribution over the Net needs a little extra thought than a printed version – but also gives you greater freedom. For example, you can include hyperlinks to other press release or background information within the electronic press release, making it considerably easier for a journalist to find all the related information. If you refer to your annual report, for example, add a hyperlink to the report to make it easy to access. Similarly, you can add a link with contact e-mail address information that provides a journalist with a one-click way of sending a message.

In the same way that newsletters (see page 46) can be sent as formatted or plain text, there are two ways of writing a press release for e-mail distribution. You can design a highly formatted page (using HTML commands as when you design a webpage) or you can stick to a plain text message. If you are sending out press releases to unknown journalists, use a simple plain text format. Almost all of the latest e-mail programs, such as Microsoft Outlook, support formatted HTML messages, but the majority of Net users still use older software that does not.

If you are creating a plain text message, you can still reference images – illustrating a product or person – by including hyperlinks to your website media section where you've stored the pictures in a webpage. If you are sending a formatted e-mail that lets you insert image files, try to use tiny representative versions (called thumbnails) of any picture to save time for the journalist when they download their e-mail. You can link these thumbnails to a bigger, higher-resolution version that's again stored on your website.

guidelines for press releases

▓ Create an e-mail template for your press releases (using HTML formatting tags if appropriate) and use this to create all your e-mail and Web-based releases.
▓ Include a section within your website dedicated to press needs – a virtual press office that includes company background, press releases, case studies and contact details.

▓ Use hyperlinks within online press releases to help reporters access related sites and files.

▓ To create formatted messages, use your wordprocessor (such as Word or WordPerfect) to create your press release then export it as an HTML file.

▓ Store your past press releases (preferably in formatted HTML format) on your website as a library of press information.

▓ To extend your coverage of press, try a specialist distribution agency service (see the Directory).

▓ Once you establish a relationship with a journalist, send personalised e-mails when you can (but turn off your contact managing software's smart features that might turn 'Michael' into 'Mike').

▓ Make sure that you know magazine or newspaper lead times – the delivery might be fast, but take into account lead times if pressing for coverage.

▓ If you use a Net-based press release agency, choose one that correctly filters contacts – some business titles don't print personnel news, some only print product reviews.

▓ If the press release is long, add a summary at the top with hyperlinks to the sections of the main document (to save scrolling) and repeat any contact details top and bottom.

▓ Separate out large images using hyperlinks to give the journalist the option of downloading the files.

▓ Don't send too many nagging e-mails following an e-mail press release – delivery is reliable and it'll arrive directly on the reporter's desktop.

▓ Make sure that your press activity coincides with your website going live – don't promote or refer people to a site that's still under construction!

distributing a press release

E-mail is an ideal way to send out a press release – it's cheap, fast, efficient and delivers direct to the journalist's desk. First, you'll need to create a mailing list of e-mail addresses. Most magazines and newspapers often have a standard format for their e-mail addresses, for example 'firstname.lastname@myMagazine.com'; check the magazine's masthead for a clue, or a newspaper's website that might provide a reporter's e-mail address. Similarly, television and radio programme websites often include biographies of reporters and an e-mail address. Many columnists and commentators have their own websites – search for these using a standard search engine, such as Excite (www.excite.com) or AltaVista (www.altavista.com). Lastly, you could turn to your paper files and check the business cards from your contacts – or simply telephone and ask for their e-mail address!

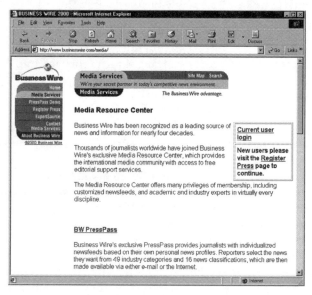

Figure 10.2 BusinessWire offers a comprehensive press release distribution service

To distribute messages, import the list of e-mail addresses into either your e-mail program's mailing list feature or your contact manager. Alternatively, you could turn to a virtual press agency that can take over the job of selecting journalists, magazines, newspapers and press agencies for your release before actually distributing your information to this group. Two of the biggest press release distribution companies are BusinessWire (www.businesswire.com) and PR Newswire (www.prnewswire.com). Both will, for a fee, distribute your electronic press release to a selection of thousands of media contacts and online agencies.

Some of these distribution companies specialise in a particular topic area. Some companies work with plain text e-mails, others will distribute video clips, sound files and the text. Costs for the service vary according to subject and number of contacts, but generally vary between $150 and $500 per job. Here are some of the main agencies online:

- BusinessWire   www.businesswire.com
- Internet Wire   www.internetwire.com
- Internet News Bureau   www.newsbureau.com
- PRNewswire   www.prnewswire.com
- URLwire   www.urlwire.com
- Xpress Press   www.xpresspress.com

public relations

The one thing that's worse than letters to your customer complaints department are customer complaints in a public forum. If a customer finds that your product is faulty or that your service is hopeless, they could complain directly to you, and some will. However, for the aggrieved customer, it's more satisfying to complain in a public forum. TV, radio and magazines are effective but hard to get into. The simplest way is to complain on the Internet in public discussion groups and newsgroups (see Chapter 8 for information on using these forums).

Take the time to monitor the newsgroups that cover your niche area and reply promptly and courteously to any complaints or problems that are posted about your products or company. Try to avoid starting an argument in a public forum. Instead, try to settle the complaint quickly and efficiently. If a product is really faulty, reply that you have passed this on to the product design department and manufacturing sections. Ask the key staff to add their findings to the newsgroup. This sort of immediate, personal response shows that your company is ready to listen to complaints and do something about them.

If you see a posting criticising terrible service, post a note that you will find out what happened – and follow up as quickly as possible with the answer. If you are at fault, offer the user a replacement product or your standard customer service. Don't forget that, like consumer TV shows, newsgroups are scanned by millions of your potential or existing customers.

customer service

The arrival of E-commerce and online shops has benefited many consumers, providing a wider choice and lower prices. But it has also led to a dramatic increase in complaints about customer service. Just because you have spent a fortune setting up an online shop rather than a traditional high-street shop does not mean that your responsibilities to the customer are any different. Websites covering bad businesses and sites and forums covering trading standards have sprouted up to give customers a chance to air their views on delivery, price, quality of product and aftercare. Make sure that you

Figure 10.3 The Net gives consumers power – BizRate lets them rate online shops

provide a dedicated e-mail address – and section on your website – for customer service questions. And answer them quickly! In the same way that the Internet empowers companies to reach a far wider audience, it also lets consumers set up pressure groups, websites and forums against a company or its products.

Look at the better-business websites, listed below, that provide guidelines on doing business on the net while offering good service. If you get something wrong, try to sort it out quickly and effectively – or your company can very quickly end up in one of the online blacklists of shopping sites to avoid.

bad-business and better-business websites

▓ Bad, Better and Best Businesses Bulletin Board
  www.webbbox.com
▓ Better Business Bureau   www.bbb.org
▓ BizRate   www.bizrate.com
▓ Internet Advocacy Center   www.consumeradvocacy.com
▓ National Fraud Information Center
  www.fraud.org
▓ Public Eye   www.thepubliceye.com/
                                review.htm
▓ WebAssured.com   www.webassured.com

consumer awareness websites

▓ Consumers' Association   www.which.net
▓ MasterCard Shop Smart   www.mastercard.com/shopsmart
▓ TRUSTe Privacy Program   www.truste.org

customer support

Most companies devote considerable resources to their customer support centres; some staff offer pre-sales service and advise potential customers on the best products, other staff handle practical or technical questions from customers about how to install, use or upgrade a product. If your customer profile suggests that they have access to the Internet, you will find that a section of your website devoted to solving common problems cuts calls to the support centres. High-technology companies (particularly software developers) often have websites that have far more on customer support, FAQs, discussion groups, technical tips and tricks, upgrades and add-ons than about the original product.

If you plan to use the Net for customer support, the first item to add to your website is an FAQ (frequently asked questions) file. This contains a list of the most frequently asked questions about your products and the answers. Your support staff can provide a list of common questions of the 'my widget won't do this' or 'does it plug in here' style. Make sure that you keep the format and tone friendly and make it searchable; you can include all the information in one webpage. If the FAQ grows, structure and refine the document or convert it to a searchable database. Place links to this section of the site on the home page and near the customer support contact details, suggesting that visitors read the FAQ before phoning. One step up from a simple FAQ is a knowledge base, a database full of tips, ideas, solutions to problems and other information about your products. This covers more advanced questions and practical ways to use your products.

To provide a more interactive environment, set up a discussion group, bulletin board or mailing list (see page 30) to let users ask questions and swap ideas. Make sure that someone from marketing or support monitors the forum and answers any questions directed to the company.

Lastly, provide direct e-mail links to your support staff – use a personal or named e-mail address rather than just 'support @mycompany.com'. If you get swamped with e-mails, use the auto-responder feature of your e-mail software (Outlook supports this as a message rule) that automatically generates a message back to the customer acknowledging receipt of their question and telling them that it will be dealt with within the next 24 hours.

research and study

The Internet can transform the way in which you plan and research your marketing strategy. It provides a vast library of generally free reference material that can help you make the right decisions. Unfortunately, the Web is so vast, with over a billion pages of information, that it's very easy to get lost or simply waste time trying to find the information you need.

The Internet is packed with statistical data, research, background information, reports, news and user comment information – and it can all be searched for free. Some websites will charge you for their information (normally specialist information such as company credit ratings or focus group meetings), but almost all the other sources of information are free to access. Here are some of the things you can do online:

- Access government databases that contain demographic information.
- Scan telephone directories that list business and personal names and addresses.
- Read the latest marketing research papers.
- Check information about travel, airlines, hotels and conventions.
- Keep track of spending patterns by consumers – and other companies.
- Market test your concepts with virtual focus groups.
- Search background information, such as annual reports or dictionaries.
- Ask members of the public for their opinions on your strategy.
- Search databases of archived newspaper and magazine articles.

- Keep abreast of the news – about the media, industry and the world.
- Access a vast library of user comments, requests and gossip about your type of services or products.
- Monitor real-time information pages that update their contents every few seconds (such as a share price).
- Read articles providing advice and expertise.

A lot of the information online is written by knowledgeable enthusiasts as well as by respected companies, but there's plenty written by amateurs whose information is likely to be neither accurate nor reliable. Try to use just the established sources and you'll avoid the contentious junk from opinionated users.

consumer research and focus groups

When you're planning a new product or campaign, you might wish that you could test out your theory on a small, select, but representative group of people. Companies with the biggest budgets can afford to pay specialist companies to carry out market research and testing with focus groups, but most companies can't afford this type of research. The Internet can help: use an online instant-response marketing research company and they'll pass your concept on to hundreds or thousands of viewers for a fast, low-cost and very useful consensus on whether you've got the right choice of colour, price or if the name is awful. Pay a company such as Greenfield Online (www.greenfield.com) and you'll get the views of thousands of people within minutes.

The alternative to this fee-based and rather traditional focus group format is the DIY approach. Instead of using a marketing company to do this background research and response work for you, you can save money and do much of it yourself by careful – very careful – use of newsgroups (see also page 132). Before you use newsgroups for any sort of market research, make sure that you understand the ground rules: for example, very few groups allow any sort of business message or product plug. Do this and you'll ruin your company's reputation with the group's audience.

The best approach is to use newsgroups as a way of listening to your customers and potential contacts for response to a product (your own or a rival's). Many of the newsgroups are job or product specific: find those that match your company's area of interest and you can get to the opinions of your target audience. You can find the perfect newsgroup using a specialist search engine such as Deja (www.deja.com).

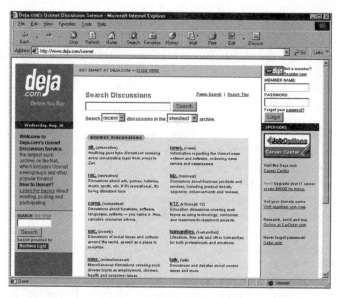

Figure 11.1   Find a newsgroup with specialist search tool Deja

When you have found a selection of newsgroups that you think might be useful, keep a daily watch on the messages, questions and complaints posted to the groups. You'll soon start to find out what this group of consumers is looking for, approves of and is irritated by. It's a slow, low-key, but effective way to get consumer feedback.

research the competition

Whatever your marketing plans – whether you are building up to a new product launch or devising a campaign to remind potential customers of an existing product – you need to know what the competition is, how it's perceived and its weaknesses. For example, if you are a dictionary publisher, is it worth going to the considerable effort of creating a newsletter, setting up a mailing list and spending money on an information-based website if your competitor in this niche market has already done all of this for its online marketing campaign? Hopefully, your competitor's plans have a flaw that yours avoid and, better still, your competitors might have missed this medium altogether.

More realistically, it's likely that your competitors will be as established as you are in their online marketing efforts. Do they have a website that accepts banner advertising? If so, can you get a rate card to find out the costs and, more importantly, a breakdown of their visitor analysis (provided for potential advertisers)? This could give you an idea if your site is performing as well as expected.

You can use the Net to find out if your competitors have established links with trade organisations or with other companies – often indicated by a link swap on their websites. One of the simplest ways to find websites that contain a link to another site is to use the AltaVista search engine (www.altavista.com) and type in the full address of the site you're interested in, for example 'www.myCompany.co.uk'. You'll see a list of any sites that have links to this site.

Your competitors might have set up a free information site away from their main branded site; for example Pfizer has its own corporate site but also runs sites providing information for allergy sufferers (one of its product lines offers allergy relief). The simplest way to search for other sites owned by the company is to use WebSitez (www.websitez.com) to search for websites listed by the company that owns the domain name.

searching

If you are searching for information, researching a new campaign or trying to find advice, most users go straight to the Web. But don't forget that newsgroups and mailing lists (see Chapter 8) are great if you want to listen to people talking and complaining about products – they could be your products.

How do you find what you want? There are millions of webpages and you'll need plenty of help to hunt out a site that's relevant. The best way to start to find information is to use an online search tool.

Figure 11.2 Business magazine *Inc.* provides a business-specific library for research

One of the best places to start looking for marketing or business information is at one of the portals (a big site that acts as a springboard to the rest of the Web). Some are based around a well-known business magazine, such as *Inc.* (www.inc.com), *Fortune* (www. fortune.com) or *Fast Company* (www.fastcompany.com), others are just information portals that gather together data from hundreds of other specialist business sites. You'll find a good selection of the top portals in the Directory, page 158.

To find a webpage that contains particular information about something you want to know, you'll need to use a search engine – a special site that provides an index of other website addresses listed according to key words and descriptions in the original page. Type in a word or phrase and you'll see a list of websites and their addresses matching your search request. As usual, the Internet provides plenty of choice, with hundreds of different sites that help you find other relevant sites and information (the main search engines are all listed in the Directory, page 157). You will also find a great range of businesses in specialist business directories such as TheBiz (www.thebiz.co.uk) or BizWeb (www.bizweb.com).

If you've tried a business directory or portal and still can't find what you're looking for, then you'll need to use your favourite general-purpose search engine such as Excite or Lycos – or, better still, use a metasearch tool. A metasearch website asks you to type in a question that it then automatically submits to all the main search engines and directories; finally, it filters the answers for relevance and presents you with a manageable list of answers. Sites like Google (www.google.com), Dogpile (www.dogpile.com), All-in-One (allonesearch.com) and MetaCrawler (www.metacrawler.com) are great for research to find the perfect marketing site. You get the benefit of all the search engines without the bother of visiting each one in turn.

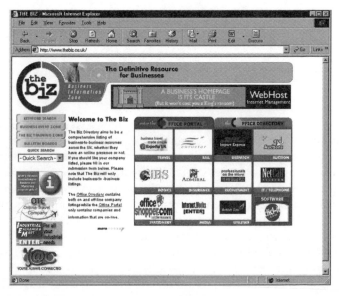

Figure 11.3 TheBiz directly helps you find a business online

Lastly, if you prefer to trust the opinions of a real human editor rather than a website's designer, turn to directory sites such as LookSmart (www.looksmart.com) or About (www.about.com), which both use editors to write mini reviews of each site together with useful general guides to a subject.

power searching

Whatever type of search you want to carry out, you don't want the results cluttered up with thousands of hobby or enthusiast sites, the perennial problem with general Internet searches. A simple search for 'broker' will display thousands of hits to everything from yacht brokers to power brokers. To limit the results you see, you'll need to start using the 'power' search features that are part of all search engines and will help you refine your search. These usually work by 'filtering' selections through one or more different criteria, defined by 'search expressions'.

To improve your searching without too much fuss, try a friendly search engine, such as HotBot (www.hotbot.com). It lets you quickly and easily define a complex search expression by choosing words that must or must not be matched. Simply click on the pull-down menus to create your search expression: it's really very easy to specify a complicated search that finds sites offering marketing advice on targeting Brazil, but not sites about travel to Brazil.

If HotBot is not your usual search engine, you will have to use a rather less friendly notation system to refine your queries. Almost all the search engines, including Yahoo! and Excite, let you refine your query using '+' and '−' symbols. If you put a '+' sign in front of a word, it means the word must be matched, and the '−' works in the opposite way. So our previous query would be entered as 'marketing +advice +Brazil −travel'. Some search engines prefer to use Boolean operators (the words AND, OR, NOT, usually in capitals), which work in a similar way to the '+' and '−' signs. For example, with Boolean logic, our example would read 'marketing AND advice AND Brazil NOT travel'.

As you sift through your results, you'll soon realise that the search engine is looking for all your words in any order on the webpage. The next step to power status is to match an exact expression. If you want to search for a particular phrase, enclose the words within double quote marks. For example, if you want to find sites covering ways to design a banner advertisement, you enclose the words within quotes: "design banner advertisement".

Often, you'll want to search for sites that are similar to one you've already found. A quick way of doing this is to use a little-used feature in the latest Microsoft and Netscape browsers. When you've found a site that's interesting, click on the 'Options/Show Related Sites' menu or 'What's related' button to see a list of sites covering the same subject. This is not always very reliable, since it relies on a central database to match similar sites, but it can produce interesting results.

newsgroups for research

Newsgroups are an often overlooked but very useful research reference medium that provides real-life comments, reactions and questions from consumers. Some newsgroups cover specific products (normally high-tech computer products), but others will cover an area of interest rather than a specific product. By reading newsgroups you can get immediate feedback about the customers' view on the subject, their likes, dislikes and requests. See Chapter 8 for information on using newsgroups.

To find the newsgroups that cover your business area you can use specialist search engines that list newsgroups and the messages within each group. If you want to search all newsgroups for particular key words, you can use one of the main search engines that covers newsgroups, such as AltaVista (www.altavista.com). Alternatively, use a specialist tool such as Deja (www.deja.com) or Tile.Net (www.tile.net), which store archives of messages posted to newsgroups and let you search for groups and messages.

Rather than searching archive material, you can monitor a particular newsgroup. Your newsreader will have a list of all the newsgroups available (new groups are added every day); use the list of available newsgroups to find one that matches your area of interest, alternatively, use Deja (www.deja.com) to find a newsgroup based on its content.

global business research

If you are planning to expand or revise your strategy in an overseas export market, the Web is the perfect research tool. It's a vast library of information, data, statistics, opinion and informed reports that together provide everything you need to research, plan and execute a new push to a different country. You can find everything from government reports to partner companies, new offices and local experts – or simply a guide to local business etiquette.

One of the best first steps is to look at the reports produced by the British Council (www.britcoun.org) or your own government trade department. These generally also include lists of potential contacts, forms that list official requests for tender from government departments and (as with the British Council) a daily e-mail service to keep you in touch with niche trade sectors. Oddly, there's one country that has little information to help potential importers – the US. This is because the majority of the Internet is centred on the US, so it assumes that most people online must also be American, hence they're looking for export markets outside the US.

To help provide marketing and general business advice on a particular export market, look to one of the general business portals – their information tends to be split between marketing and physical problems such as shipping and customs. Look in the Directory, page 158, for some of the best sites to help you get started.

You can use the Internet to provide basic feasibility studies on the market, to check potential customer base, per capita income, competing products and so on. It's worth looking at sites from global organisations such as the World Bank (www.worldbank.com) since a grant from this organisation can (and often does) transform a niche sector within a country.

Lastly, if you've decided to target a market and it's worth a visit, check on sites such as Travlang (www.travlang.com) to get a basic understanding of the language, culture and business etiquette before you arrive.

marketing talk

There is far more than glossy websites available online. One of the most popular ways to use the Net is to discuss things: marketing strategies, ad campaigns, prices, staff, ideas, contacts, complaints, tips or just worries. The Net is very good at bringing together large, dispersed groups of users who can meet in one place and discuss just about anything. There are three basic types of place on the Net where you can meet up and chat:

- Web forums or discussion areas
- mailing lists
- newsgroups (also called Usenet).

For marketing and business discussions, you'll probably find that the discussion groups that form part of marketing or business magazines and advice websites prove the most useful, but it's well worth touring the mailing lists and newsgroups to see what's going on.

E-zines

E-zines (or newsletters) aren't interactive discussion groups – the information flows from the publisher to you. However, they are often very useful, interesting and even influential. The hard part is trying to find where they are and how to subscribe. Almost all are delivered by e-mail, on a daily, weekly or monthly basis. There are very few places that try to keep an index of the zines on the Web; try the following to find your perfect match:

- Ezine-Universe   www.ezine-universe.com
- HotWired   www.hotwired.com/zines/
- Zinos   www.zinos.com

Figure 12.1   Ezine-Universe is one of the few sites that helps you find an E-zine

discussion groups

One of the most popular features of many business and specialist marketing websites is a discussion group. Almost all of the websites for the major business magazines – such as *Inc.* (www.inc.com) – include a section for discussion groups. Any visitor can join in the discussion, although you may be asked to register first, for free. Almost all discussion groups originated in the pre-Internet days of bulletin-board systems such as CompuServe (www.compuserve.com), AOL (www.aol.com) and CIX (www.cix.co.uk). All three still offer a very wide range of discussion groups (called forums), but you can access them only if you're a subscriber.

Using online discussion groups is easy and is all done with your Web browser. When you visit a site, such as *Fast Company* (www.fastcompany.com/community/), you'll see a list of the titles of the previous few messages. To read a message, double click on its title. If a message has a reply, it should display a tiny plus sign just to the left. Click on this and you'll see the original message and all the related replies. You can add a reply to a message or create a new message.

The hardest part of discussion groups is to find a good one. There's no real central index of groups within websites; flip to the Directory, page 159, where we have included a list of sites to help get you started.

mailing lists

Mailing lists are a great way to distribute messages to a group of people with the same interests. They are a perfect way to keep up to date with a particular subject, special-interest group or colleagues. Unlike Web-based discussion groups, mailing lists work through your normal e-mail program. The group is simply a collection of e-mail addresses of subscribers managed automatically by a special program, normally called a list server. When you want to post a message to the group, send an e-mail to the list server's e-mail address; your message is then distributed to everyone else on the list.

Mailing lists are one of the oldest uses for the Internet – they were developed by academics in the early days, before the Web took hold and when e-mail was the main use for the Net. There are now tens of thousands of mailing lists covering just about every subject you might want to know about. And finding your ideal mailing list is easy thanks to the range of search engines that let you search a database of mailing lists organised by subject. Three of the main search engines are Liszt (www.liszt.com), CataList (www.lsoft.com/lists/listref.html) and Tile.net (www.tile.net) – all three will help you find a list and get details about how to subscribe. Alternatively, visit the dedicated websites that lets users set up their own mailing list for free, for example eGroups (www.egroups.com).

newsgroups

Newsgroups are a vast collection of forums for free speech and provide one of the most active areas of the Internet. They work just like an office noticeboard – anyone can post a message that can then be read by anyone else. You might not like everything that's said in them, but they are great places to get feedback, opinions and research. To start using newsgroups (sometimes called the Usenet) you need a newsreader program. All the main Web browser applications include a newsreader. Microsoft's reader is part of its Outlook Express program (which also manages your e-mail), which can be downloaded from the www.microsoft.com site. If you prefer to try something other than the default Microsoft product, look in the Directory, page 162, for a list of other free readers.

Newsgroups are divided into seven broad categories, called hierarchies, which differentiate the groups very roughly by type of subject. In addition to seven main categories, there is an eighth category called 'alt', which contains a wide and wild range of newsgroups (and is generally responsible for the lewd reputation of newsgroups).

Your ISP will have a special computer dedicated to storing some of the messages that form the Usenet. This new server computer probably stores the last few day's worth of messages from most (but not all) the newsgroups. You'll need the address of the news server (often something like 'news.btinternet.com') to configure your newsgroup reader.

Newsgroups work in a very different way to Web-based discussion groups. There's no single computer that stores all the newsgroups. Instead, the news servers at every ISP swap information to ensure that they are always up to date. If you post a message, it will appear instantly in the newsgroup stored on your ISP's news server, but it will take a few seconds before it is copied to all the other news servers in the area then, gradually, your message will automatically be copied to all the news servers across the world.

finding a newsgroup

When you first connect to your news server, your software will download the current list of newsgroups. You can browse through, looking for something that sounds interesting, or use your reader's filter function to narrow down the list to group titles that contain a particular word.

A better way to find a newsgroup that's interesting is to use a specialist search engine, such as Deja (www.deja.com) or Tile.Net (www.tile.net), to search through the archives of newsgroup messages – you'll soon see which newsgroups are relevant.

using a newsgroup

Your newsgroup reader software looks rather like a standard e-mail program: on the left there's usually a list of the newsgroups and on the right you'll see the title line of the latest postings. Click on the title and the full message is displayed.

Reading newsgroup messages when you're connected to the Internet is ideal, but, depending on your ISP and the type of account you have, your phone bill could rocket. A more efficient alternative is to download all the new messages from your selected newsgroups, then log off and read them offline. If you post any replies, wait until you've read all the messages, then dial up and send off your new messages.

It's easy to blunder when typing your first newsgroup posting, so make life a little easier on yourself and use one of the newsgroups dedicated to newcomers trying out the system: alt.test and misc.test.

Lastly, consider your identity when you post your messages. Every message posted includes the sender's e-mail address. It's up to you, the sender, to decide whether to supply a real or a fake e-mail address. Most newsgroup users really don't want to be identified, so they provide a false e-mail address. In fact, this isn't the crime you might imagine, but a perfectly reasonable response to a major problem. Unscrupulous mail-shot companies trawl through newsgroups picking up the e-mail addresses and adding these to a mailing list that's then sold on. You can guarantee that, if you post a message under your real e-mail address, you'll soon be bombarded with junk mail and spam. One solution to get around this problem is to setup a free e-mail account (see Directory, page 162) and use this for newsgroup postings.

getting online

Before you can start using the Internet, you've got to get connected and get online. This section is a basic guide to getting your computer – or your office network – online. If you're already online, you can ignore this section and simply use the rest of the book to improve your marketing strategy online.

For most users and companies, the gateway to the Internet is via a specialist communications company, called an Internet service provider (ISP). The ISP provides a telephone access number for your modem, ISDN or ADSL connection together with a user name and password. Once you have installed the software that you need to connect and use the Internet, you will need to configure it to call the ISP's access number and make the connection.

Once you're online, you can browse the Web, send and receive electronic mail and publish your own website. If it all sounds rather complex, don't worry. Thankfully, almost all new computers now come with all the extra software you need pre-installed, and ISPs generally send out custom CD-ROMs with automated installation guides, ensuring that you get online with just a few clicks.

If you want to publish your own website, you'll need an Internet service provider that can host your site and let you use your own domain name and advanced features such as adding a database.

choosing an ISP

You need to set up an account with an ISP to provide your path to the Internet. This works as an intermediary, providing a local telephone number to dial in and connect to its main computers, which form part of the Internet. Only the very biggest sites or corporations link directly to the Internet; everyone else makes use of an ISP and leaves it to manage the complex network connections.

Essentially there are just two types of ISP: one charges a fee and the other is free. Free ISPs are tempting, but are geared to home users and often don't support the extra features you'll need to build a business website. Some ISPs now even provide free telephone calls to subscribers, particularly in the evening or weekends. A couple of companies – AOL and CompuServe – offer global access numbers, which are a boon if you or your colleagues travel on business and want to stay in touch. However, for most companies you simply want a fast, reliable and low-cost connection to the Internet. One of the best ways to choose an ISP is to use the league tables produced by the online Internet magazines that rank different ISPs by speed and features. Visit *.net* (www.netmag.co.uk), *Internet Magazine* (www.internet-magazine.com) or *Internet.Works* (www.iwks.com).

To pick up your e-mail messages, try a service such as Mail2Web (www.mail2web.com). This lets you access your mailbox via a Web browser (vist your local Internet café) – you can't use this for most office e-mail network systems, but it's an alternative to a full AOL or Compuserve Subscription.

An ISP provides the connection and route to the Internet, but you don't have to use it for all your Net jobs. There are many Web hosting companies that specialise in providing Web space on which to store your website pages; you'll still need an ISP to get online, but the Web hosting company might be able to provide a better deal for your Web space requirements, simply because they don't have the overhead of managing telephone connections for users' modems.

getting on the Internet

You can connect just about any computer to the Internet, from a high-powered workstation to a pocket organiser. You don't even need a computer to get the benefits of the Net. If you have a mobile phone or pager, you can use this to receive information from some websites. And if your office has a network installed, you can link everyone on the network to the Internet very easily, although you'll probably need extra hardware and software.

If you're connecting just one computer, the easiest way is to use a modem and a normal phone line. If you plan to make a lot of use of the Net, or if you're connecting the entire office, you'll soon get complaints about slow speed from users and you should install a faster link such as ISDN or ADSL (asymmetric digital subscriber line). In the UK, there is a small-business-friendly version of ISDN called Business Highway, but with the arrival of ADSL this begins to look like an expensive solution.

ISDN provides a relatively fast connection, but the technology of ADSL is proving hard to beat. You get a permanent connection to the Internet for a fixed monthly subscription of around £50. It's many times faster than ISDN and can be a lot cheaper in call charges, making it an ideal route for offices and high-traffic users. If you do sign up for ADSL, make sure that you also install some form of firewall – it is far more susceptible to attack than standard dial-up connections such as ISDN.

To share your high-speed link across all the computers in the office, you'll need to install a special device called a router. This connects the office network to your ISDN or ADSL line and automatically manages the connection to the Net any time someone on the local office network starts a Web browser or e-mail application. A specialist business ISP will be able to supply all the equipment you require, pre-configured, to connect everyone on your network to the Net.

why it's always so slow

The Internet sometimes seems to grind to a standstill but, just as unexpectedly, it can zing along at a cracking rate. The performance you see has little to do with your computer, more to do with the type of connection, and is far more related to the traffic jams elsewhere in the world on the Net.

The speed of your connection (modem, ISDN or ADSL link) determines how fast you can transfer information to and from your computer, but you are still just as likely to hit congestion on the backbone (the main motorway of data flow that links your ISP to all the other providers). As more users log in at peak time, the motorway chokes up – so it is best to avoid early evening or your local-time equivalent to when the US wakes up.

office Net policy

Connect everyone in your office to the Net and there's the chance that they'll all suddenly start playing online games, ordering their shopping, spending hours in chat rooms or viewing pornography. The Internet is supposed to improve productivity, but instead you might suddenly find that productivity collapses – unless you provide a firm office policy and install a way of policing it.

If you connect your office network to the Internet, there are two new problems you will have to deal with:

- colleagues accessing inappropriate sites or wasting time playing games
- misusing the channel to send unsuitable, unwanted or libellous e-mail messages.

The first problem is relatively simple to manage and depends a great deal on your office policy. If you don't mind employees booking their holidays online, ordering their shopping or visiting porn sites, then there's nothing to worry about. However, it would be sensible to draw up a list of things you would rather employees did not do. Make sure everyone knows this and respects it. If you want to prevent any infringement of these rules, you could install management software to shut down a user's session on the Net as soon as they try to access a forbidden site, and send a warning message to a supervisor.

The second problem is far more difficult to solve, let alone define for your office policy. It covers the way your colleagues send information over the Net, particularly by e-mail. As a writing medium, e-mail encourages sloppy writing, gossip and far worse. In the US, recent court cases have found companies liable if an employee sends unwanted, libellous or sexually provocative e-mail messages – even if they were meant as a joke.

E-mail is also particulary good for quick personal messages, party planning and even job applications. However, it's hard to set down the most basic of rules covering the use of e-mails. Some big companies now install message-scanning utilities (see the Directory, page 164) that run on the office network server and look for key words in any e-mail message. If a message contains words such as 'sex', 'secret' or 'job application', the entire message can be stopped before it leaves the office.

setting up the software

To use the Internet you need to install and configure special software on your computer to manage the connection and to let you view webpages and read e-mail. However, all the software is normally pre-installed on new computers and most ISPs will also send you a CD-ROM with similar pre-configured software ready to install. If you have a CD-ROM from your ISP, insert it in the drive and follow the instructions. Both Windows 98 and 2000 as well as Macintosh OS 9 include an automated installation process that leads you through a set of simple, step-by-step procedures to configure the pre-installed software. Follow either process and you will end up with all the software you need, ready to connect to the Net.

Once you sign up with an ISP you'll receive a user name, a password, an e-mail address and the telephone access number you use to connect and get online. If you register with AOL, CompuServe or an ISP that supplies a complete installation kit, the software automatically generates a user name and supplies the access phone number ready for your computer to dial.

As well as these basic pieces of information, you'll be sent a list of settings that you need to send and receive e-mail messages and access newsgroups. The Microsoft Windows or Macintosh OS 9 Internet installers both take you step by step through the process of typing these settings into the correct section of the software. Again, if you've subscribed to AOL, CompuServe or an ISP that provides a complete automated installation package, these settings will be filled in automatically.

To start using the Web, double click on the Web browser icon on your desktop (or the AOL or CompuServe icon, if you've signed up with these providers) and the software will start. It automatically dials the telephone access number, supplies your user name and password and sets up your connection to the Net.

When you're connected to the Net, Windows will display a tiny icon in the bottom right-hand corner of the screen with two green squares linked. If you see this, you're online. The squares should flash bright green to show that information is being transferred. The top square is the distant computer at the ISP and the bottom square represents your computer. If you're connecting via a network, you won't see this icon. With a Macintosh system, the Apple icon in the top left-hand corner will alternate with the icon for the Remote Access program that dials the Net for you.

Once you are connected, your browser automatically displays a nominated webpage, called its 'home page' (normally your ISP's main page). You can change this easily so that you see your favourite financial page, newspaper or even the latest prices for your portfolio of shares by selecting the Tools/Internet Options menu in Internet Explorer or Edit/Preferences in Navigator and clicking on the button USE CURRENT PAGE to automatically insert the current site address. Next time you start the browser, it will display your favourite webpage.

browsing the Web

To visit a website, you have to type in the website's full address (called its URL) in the address box that's just under the menu bar in the top left-hand corner of your Web browser. This is probably already displaying the address of the current home page. Just type over this, for example 'www.wilsonweb.com' for the excellent marketing portal, Wilson Internet. You don't need to type in the initial 'http://' part of an address – the browser fills this in for you. Press RETURN and your browser tries to find and display the page. If it cannot find the site or page, you'll see an error message; check that you have typed the address in correctly and try again.

The main area of the Web browser displays the webpage. Hyper-links are normally displayed as blue underlined text. As you move your pointer over a link you'll see it change to a pointing hand icon. Click and you'll jump to a new page. You can display several separate copies of the browser window by pressing CTRL-N (or APPLE-N on a Mac). Each window works independently, so you can view separate sites or pages in each.

electronic mail

It's no exaggeration to say that electronic mail will totally transform your communications. You can receive marketing tips, newsletters or news headlines via e-mail, or keep in touch with your colleagues, customers and professional contacts. To send or receive electronic mail messages you need an e-mail program and an Internet connection to send off the messages. If you have a relatively new computer, it will already have e-mail software pre-installed as part of the Web browser software supplied by Microsoft or Netscape.

If you're on an office network, you should check with your IT manager which is the preferred software for your installation. Alternatively, if your ISP has sent you a CD-ROM with pre-configured software, you can use this instead. If you are configuring the software pre-installed on your computer (that is, not pre-configured and supplied by your ISP), then make sure that you have your e-mail address, user name, password and the address of the computer that manages e-mail at the ISP (usually two names called, for example, 'smtp.demon.co.uk' and 'pop.demon.co.uk').

Don't forget that e-mail is sent as plain text – if anyone intercepts the message, they can read it. To prevent this, protect sensitive e-mails by encrypting the contents. Use the built-in feature in your e-mail program or, for ultimate security, use the PGP system (www.pgp.com).

e-mail standards

Most e-mail users work with one of the standard Internet e-mail systems, normally provided by their ISP. When you sign up, you configure your computer to send and receive mail messages via the ISP's central mail server computer. This computer temporarily stores any incoming mail until you go online and download the messages to your computer. If you send a message, your e-mail software transfers it to the server, which in turn sends it over the Internet to its destination.

E-mail is normally sent using a system called SMTP (simple mail transfer protocol) and received using a different system called POP3 (post office protocol-3). Almost all e-mail programs support this SMTP/POP3 mix of standards. Most decent ISPs will provide pre-configured software in their starter packs. If not, you'll be sent the addresses of the ISP's mail server: normally one for incoming, one for outgoing mail. A new, more flexible e-mail standard is slowly growing in popularity. Called IMAP (Internet message access protocol), it lets you read your mail even if you're away from your computer. Almost all the latest e-mail software programs support this new standard but, unless you work in a big company, it's unlikely that you'll use this feature immediately.

Web-based e-mail

So far, we've covered e-mail that you send and receive with a special program running on your computer. It's fast, flexible and still the most popular way of managing mail messages. However, there's an alternative way of managing your e-mail, using a program that runs on a remote website and is accessed via a webpage, displayed in your standard Web browser. You can send and receive standard mail messages and have your own address, but have the advantage of accessing your messages from anywhere in the world that has access to the Web – an Internet café, library or work.

Perhaps the best feature is that you can get a Web-based e-mail account for free from hundreds of different suppliers (such as Yahoo!, Excite, MSN and CometMail – see the Directory, page 162). Users who don't have a computer at home often set up a Web-based e-mail address, and it's also a good way to create a personal e-mail address that doesn't clog up your office account.

addressing e-mail

If you send a message to an e-mail address that doesn't exist, the message will come straight back again; this is called a bounce and tells you within minutes that the message could not be delivered. In most cases, the returned message will also contain extra information that tells you what went wrong – the user name might not be recognised by the server or perhaps the server is not responding at that moment.

Unfortunately, there's no complete, central directory of e-mail addresses to help you find someone's address. You've got three options: phone them and ask them, visit their company's website to see if there's a contact list or search one of the small directories of addresses that do exist (such as Yahoo! People Search at people.yahoo.com).

Almost every e-mail program lets you send messages to more than one person at a time. This is great if you want to set up a newsletter with a small circulation or simply keep colleagues in the loop about a project. There are three address panels in your e-mail program where you can enter a recipient's address:

To: will send the message to the address of the person in this panel. You can list several addresses (separated by a comma or semi-colon or space), in which case each person gets their own individual message and doesn't realise it's been sent to anyone else.

CC: (short for carbon copy) works with the 'To:' field. Type in the address of another person who should see a copy of this message. The person in the 'To:' field will be told who else has seen the message.

BCC: (short for blind carbon copy) works with the 'To:' field (and the CC: field, if you want). If you type in an address here, they'll receive a copy of the message, but the person in the 'To:' field won't know that a copy's been sent.

The basic addressing features of your e-mail software are fine if you want to setup a small-circulation newsletter with fewer than a hundred names. Any more than this and you'll find it easier to use a special mailing list program. Some contact managers, such as ACT!, Maximizer or GoldMine, have e-mail merge facilities and can handle several hundred e-mail messages per session.

The problem with both of these systems is that you are doing the work of sending a message from your desktop computer. A far more efficient way is to use special software that runs on your server computer (or your ISP's server). This has a faster link to the Net and provides a more efficient solution. You submit a list of recipients and a text file to be sent to each and the software pumps out the messages. Visit Everything E-mail (www.everything email.com) for links to dozens of mass mailing programs.

sending to fax, pager or telephone

Your e-mail messages don't have to go to another computer. You can send messages to a normal fax machine, a pager or a mobile phone (with or without WAP).

If you are travelling and only have an e-mail connection, but need to send a message to a colleague who only has a fax machine, use an e-mail–fax gateway that links the two systems. Some are free, others will charge you. The free systems tend to include a line of advertising at the bottom of each fax, but are fast and efficient. Have a look at the efficient TPC (www.tpc.int), the gaudy Zipfax site (www.zipfax.com) or the simple Oxford University site (info.ox.ac.uk/fax/).

Although the main mobile phone providers let you send text messages between phones, it's a different matter when it's Web to phone. They're all trial systems, but at the time of going to press, only Orange (www.orange.co.uk) seems to provide a consistent service, with Vodafone (www.vodafone.co.uk) promising to offer the service soon.

security and viruses

Scare stories in newspapers ensure that most companies know about the security risks of the Internet – but not all treat it as a priority. The reality is that the risks are low, but you should still take sensible precautions to protect your company's computers and local area network.

If you plan to link just one computer to the Net, the risks are minimal. However, most companies link their LAN (local area network) to the Internet and share access among users in the company. Once you connect your network to the Internet, you leave your company's computers open to relatively easy attack from a hacker. To reduce the risk, make sure that you install a firewall device that prevents access from external users.

Here are the basic security measures that you should implement:

- Install network access control software or hardware, usually a firewall. This checks any user as they try to access your network and will stop any unauthorised users – such as hackers – gaining access or viewing your local files. If you are installing a router, used to provide shared Internet access, many provide basic firewall features and prevent other Internet users and hackers gaining access to your network.
- If you have just signed up to the ADSL standard for high-speed links to the Net, you are also entering a higher-risk category. The problem with ADSL is that it is 'always on' – your computer or network is always connected to the Internet, making it an easier target for hackers. If you connect via ADSL you must fit a firewall or similar access control device.

virus attacks

Just about any file you download could contain a virus, but in reality the number of incidents is very low. However, if your PC or your company's network becomes infected, it can be very damaging – so protect your computers now. Viruses are tiny, highly sophisticated programs that take advantage of a loophole in a computer system or software application. They normally burrow into another 'carrier' file, often a computer program or sometimes an e-mail message, or a Word or Excel document (called macro viruses).

When you open or run the carrier file, the virus wakes up and does two things: first, it tries to spread to other similar files, to 'infect' them; next, it might try to wreak havoc on your computer.

Many viruses are harmless but annoying and simply spread themselves, but the majority will try to delete files, crash your hard disk or corrupt information stored in files.

You cannot catch a virus simply by downloading a file. However, if the file you download is infected with a virus, you will catch it when you open or run the file. If you download a file or receive a file via an e-mail attachment, it could also contain a virus, so you have to be particularly careful when dealing with attachments received from an unknown e-mail address.

Only a few types of file can't contain viruses, notably image files and simple webpages (however, many webpages use extra programs, called applets, to provide multimedia or special effects, and these could contain a virus).

To stop any potential problems, never open e-mail attachments from users you don't know. Always scan newly downloaded files with a special software program that can detect and remove viruses – before you open the file. Lastly, install background scanning software on the company server to ensure that the main files are protected. Two of the most popular virus detection programs are McAfee (www.mcafee.com) and Norton AntiVirus (www.symantec.com).

directory

advice for site builders

Tools, programming languages and techniques for building web-sites keep changing. Here are some of the best places dedicated to web developers:

- Builder.com   www.builder.com
- Web Pages That Suck   www.webpagesthatsuck.com
- WebDeveloper   www.webdeveloper.com
- WebMonkey   www.webmonkey.com

webpage editors

You can design a webpage with your wordprocessor, but to create complex pages it's far easier to use a specialist design program. Here are some of the best-known webpage design tools. Most let you download a trial version to try out before you buy the full software:

- Dreamweaver   www.macromedia.com
- Fusion   www.netobjects.com
- Frontpage   www.microsoft.com
- GoLive   www.adobe.com
- HotDog   www.sausage.com
- HoTMetaL   www.hotmetalpro.com

▓ PageMill	www.adobe.com
▓ Visual Page	www.symantec.com

Web databases

A database is one of the most popular features that you can add to your website, but it can be difficult. You can ask your Web space host company (or ISP) to do all the work for you, or use an off-the-shelf database product, such as FileMaker, or roll up your sleeves and use a free program from a library such as ScriptSearch.

▓ Borland	www.borland.com
▓ FileMaker Pro	www.filemaker.com
▓ Microsoft	www.microsoft.com
▓ Oracle	www.oracle.com
▓ R:Base Technologies	www.microrim.com
▓ ScriptSearch	www.scriptsearch.com

website resources

Add a little animated widget to your site or spruce up the graphics with specially designed clip-art. You'll find a whole range of extras that can improve your site – but don't use too many or it will start to look messy.

▓ ActiveX	www.microsoft.com
▓ BrowserWatch	www.browserwatch.com
▓ Clipart.com	www.clipart.com
▓ FreeScripts	www.freescripts.com
▓ Java	www.java.sun.com
▓ JavaScript	www.javascript.com
▓ Perl programming language	www.perl.org
▓ ScriptSearch	www.scriptsearch.com
▓ Shockwave	www.macromedia.com

multimedia servers

If your chairman demands a live Internet broadcast, or if you want to include video or audio clips on your website, here are some of the major players that can provide the technology:

- Media Server (Netscape)   home.netscape.com
- NetShow (Microsoft)   www.microsoft.com
- RealNetworks   www.realaudio.com
- StreamWorks (Xing)   www.xingtech.com
- WebTheater (VXtreme)   www.microsoft.com

promoting websites

Promoting your website to search engines is essential to its success. Either do this yourself by visiting each search engine in turn or use one of these automated tools to do it for you, often for a fee. Then use LinkPopularity and SearchEngineWatch to monitor the results.

- DidIt   www.did-it.com
- Exploit   www.exploit.com
- LinkPopularity   www.linkpopularity.com
- SearchEngineWatch   www.searchenginewatch.com
- Submit It   www.submit-it.com
- WebPosition   www.webposition.com

what's new and award sites

There are specialist websites that list the latest, best websites on the Net – submit your site for evaluation to the award sites. Don't forget to check magazine and newspaper sites (such as *USA Today*, www.usatoday.com), which often have their own listings for new or noteworthy sites.

- *Internet Magazine*   www.internet-magazine.com/bookmarks/
- Netscape   www.netscape.com/netcenter/new.html
- Yahoo!   www.yahoo.com/picks

measuring response and Web analysis

The key to measuring your website's success is to analyse the access logs that record every click of every visitor. Ask your Web hosting provider to supply access logs detailing who viewed what and when on your website. To make sense of the raw data, you'll need a specialist Web log analysis program – some Web hosting companies supply this for free, others only supply the data. You can buy a commercial product or use one of the shareware products on offer. Here are some of the main products and places to find out more:

- Accrue Software   www.accrue.com
- Analog   www.statslab.cam.ac.uk/~sret1/analog
- DoubleClick   www.doubleclick.com
- eHNC   www.aptex.com
- MapQuest   www.mapquest.com
- WebTrends   www.webtrends.com
- Yahoo!   dir.yahoo.com/Business_and_Economy/
  Business_to_Business/Computers/
  Software/Internet/World_Wide_Web/
  Log_Analysis_Tools/

e-mail marketing

If you want to test out e-mail marketing with a cold-call mail-out to a possible target audience, use an approved mailing list supplier, recommended by your trade organisation (such as the DMA). Here are sites that provide the lists, the software to send the messages efficiently and ideas to help make the most of the medium:

- Arial Software Campaign — www.arialsoftware.com
- Colorado Soft WorldMerge — www.coloradosoft.com
- Direct Email List Source — www.copywriter.com/lists/

- Direct e-mail marketing — www.e-target.com
- Direct Marketing Association — www.the-dma.com
- DM News — www.dmnews.com
- Eletter — www.eletter.com
- EverythingAboutEmail — www.everythingaboutemail.com

- infoUSA — www.infousa.com
- Interact — www.interact.com
- MailKing — www.messagemedia.com/solutions/mailking

- Marketing File — www.marketingfile.com
- Stamps.com — www.stamps.com
- Yahoo! — dir.yahoo.com/Business_and_Economy/Business_to_Business/Marketing_and_Advertising/Direct_Marketing/Direct_Email

renting e-mail lists

If you plan on renting an e-mail list, make sure the contacts on the list opted in to receive advertising messages. Try these specialist e-mail list brokers to start:

- Copywriter — www.copywriter.com/lists
- InBoxExpress — www.inboxexpress.com

- PostMasterDirect   www.postmasterdirect.com
- Targ-it   www.targ-it.com

banner advertising

Banner adverts can work well as a way of promoting your new website – or equally as a way of raising money to support your site. These sites will help you design an effective banner ad graphic image:

- Adbility   www.adbility.com
- AdClub   www.adclub.net
- BannerAd Network   www.banneradnetwork.com
- BannerExchange   www.bannerexchange.com
- BannerTips   www.bannertips.com
- BannerWorkz   www.bannerworkz.com
- Budget Banners   www.budget-banners.com
- Link Exchange   www.bcentral.com
- Outer Planet   www.outerplanet.com

advertising agencies

If you want to run a banner ad campaign or sell space on your website, you can negotiate this yourself or use a specialist agency. If you plan on using an agency, here are some of the main players in the banner ad field:

- Active Media Research   www.activemediaresearch.com
- DoubleClick   www.doubleclick.com
- Engage I/PRO   www.engage.com/ipro/
- WebConnect   www.webconnect.com
- WebTrack   www.webtrack.com

E-advertising

The major ad agencies all have their own websites and are all promoting their E-advertising services. If you have the budget and
need, here are some of the biggest agencies:

- Abbott Mead Vickers. BBDO — www.amvbbdo.co.uk
- Bartle Bogle Hegarty — www.bbh.co.uk
- BMP DDB — www.bmp.co.uk
- Cordiant — www.ccgww.com
- D'Arcy Masius Benton & Bowles — www.dmbb.com
- Grey — www.grey.com
- J Walter Thompson — www.jwtworld.com
- Leo Burnett — www.leoburnett.com
- Lowe Lintas — www.lowehoward-spink.co.uk
- McCann-Erickson — www.mccann.com
- Saatchi & Saatchi — wwww.saatchi-saatchi.com
- Young & Rubicam — www.yandr.com

shopping carts

To set up an online shop you'll need some type of shopping cart
software. Some companies provide a simple step-by-step route to
setting up your shop on their site, or you can install your own
software for a more complex, but more customised, solution. Here
are some of the main turnkey and custom cart providers:

- Actinic Catalog — www.actinic.com
- Cart32 — www.cart32.com
- COWS — www.cows.co.uk
- Dansie Shopping Cart — www.dansie.net
- EasyCart — www.easycart.com

FreeMerchant	www.freemerchant.com
IBM WebSphere Commerce Suite	www.ibm.com/software/ webservers/commerce/
iCat	www.icat.com
Ideal Seller	www.thevisionfactory.com
Intershop	www.intershop.com
JShop Professional	www.jshop.co.uk
JumboStore	www.jumbostore.com
Mercantec SoftCart	www.mercantec.com
Miva Merchant	www.miva.com
n2plus Synergy	www.n2plus.com
PerlShop	www.arpanet.com
SalesCart	www.salescart.com
Shopcreator	www.shopcreator.com
VIPcart	www.vipcart.com
Virginbiz	www.virginbiz.net
Yahoo! Store	store.yahoo.com

payment processing

If you want to accept credit card payments in your online shop, you'll need to use a payment processing site. These companies check and authorise card numbers in an instant. Almost all charge a fee on transactions – compare their rates with ShopForRates (www.shopforrates.com). Here are some of the main providers.

UK processing

Secure Trading	www.securetrading.com
DataCash	www.datacash.com
NetBanx	www.netinvest.co.uk/ncr/netbanx/
WorldPay	www.worldpay.com

US processing

▓ 1st American Card Service   www.1stamericancard
                                    service.com
▓ Advantage Merchant Services   www.creditcardprocessor
                                    .com
▓ American Express   www.americanexpress
                                    .com/business
▓ Authorize.Net   www.authorize.net
▓ BankAmerica Merchant Services   www.bankofamerica.com/
                                    merchantservices
▓ Charge.Com   www.charge.com
▓ Electronic Payment Processing   www.epp-inc.com
▓ ePayment Resource Center   www.epaynews.com
▓ GORealtime   www.gorealtime.com
▓ Internet Credit Network   www.creditnet.com
▓ iTransact   www.redicheck.com
▓ Mastercard Merchant Site   www.mastercard.com/
                                    merchants
▓ Open Market   www.openmarket.com
▓ Pay2See   www.pay2see.com
▓ PaylinX   www.paylinx.com

watchdogs

Consumers can fight back on the Internet using the many websites
that are designed to promote hopeless service and expose crooks.
Most also have lists of friendly shops that are recommended. Visit
these to see what to do and what not to do to keep on their good
side:

▓ Bad, Better and Best Businesses Bulletin Board
                                    www.webBbox.com
▓ Better Business Bureau   www.bbb.org
▓ BizRate   www.bizrate.com

▨ Internet Advocacy Center	www.consumer advocacy.com
▨ National Fraud Information Center	www.fraud.org
▨ Public Eye	www.thepubliceye .com/review.htm
▨ WebAssured	www.webassured .com

business to business

Now that your company is Net friendly, you'll probably start to use the Web to find trading partners. Here are some of the biggest business-to-business (B2B) directories on the Web, packed with other Web-enabled companies:

▨ 1st Global Directory	www.1stglobaldirectory.com
▨ AB Directory	www.comfind.com
▨ Asource	www.asource.com
▨ BizExpose.com	www.bizexpose.com
▨ BizWeb	www.bizweb.com
▨ Companies House	www.companieshouse.org.uk
▨ Companies Online	www.companiesonline.com
▨ dot com directory	www.dotcomdirectory.com
▨ Dow Jones Business Directory	www.businessdirectory .dowjones.com
▨ EcoMall Companies	www.ecomall.com/biz/
▨ ExpertFind	www.expertfind.com
▨ Hoover's Online	www.hoovers.com
▨ IndustryLink	www.industrylink.com
▨ Starting Point Business Categories	www.stpt.com/ channel.asp?id=1
▨ Startup Zone	www.startupzone.com
▨ The Biz	www.thebiz.co.uk
▨ VerticalNet	www.verticalnet.com
▨ ZDNet Company Finder	www.zdnet.com/ companyfinder/filters/home/

search engines and directories

If you're trying to find information somewhere on the Web, you'll need to use a search engine or directory. Search engines, such as AltaVista (www.altavista.com), try to list every site available on the Web, whereas directories, such as Yahoo! (www.yahoo.com), limit themselves to a select few hundred thousand sites. You can search their indexes for sites that might contain the information you're looking for.

About	www.about.com
AltaVista	www.altavista.co.uk
EuroSeek	www.euroseek.com
Excite	www.excite.co.uk
G.O.D.	www.god.co.uk
HotBot	www.hotbot.com
Infoseek	www.infoseek.com
LookSmart	www.looksmart.co.uk
Lycos	www.lycos.co.uk
Magellan	megellan.excite.com
Northern Light	www.northernlight.com
Scoot	www.scoot.co.uk
UKPlus	www.ukplus.com
WebCrawler	www.webcrawler.com
Yahoo!	www.yahoo.co.uk
Yell	www.yell.co.uk

metasearchers

Metasearchers are a brilliant idea that is often underused by surfers: these sites will submit your search query to dozens of search engines and directories (see above) and then filter the results to give you the most likely results.

All-in-One	www.allonesearch.com
AskJeeves	www.ask.co.uk

- DogPile   www.dogpile.com
- Google   www.google.com
- InFind   www.infind.com
- MetaCrawler www.metacrawler.com
- Search.com   www.search.com

business portals

- AllBusiness.com   www.allbusiness.com
- bCentral   www.bcentral.com
- Bloomberg   www.bloomberg.com
- EOCenter   www.eocenter.com
- FinanceWise   www.financewise.com
- Inc. Online   www.inc.com
- Killerbiz   www.killerbiz.com
- Office.com   www.office.com
- Raging Bull   www.ragingbull.com
- SmartAge   www.smartage.com
- Smart Online   www.smartonline.com
- The Biz   www.thebiz.co.uk
- Web Watch   www.businessdirectory.dowjones.com

researching export markets

If you're trying to expand into another market or country, you need statistics, information and expert advice. Use one of these specialist exporters' sites to help you understand how a particular export market works, how to tackle it and to look for local contacts to help you succeed:

- Big Emerging Markets Information Resource Page
                           www.ita.doc.gov/bems/
- British Council   www.britcoun.org
- Central Europe Online   www.centraleurope.com
- Company Annual Reports On-Line (CAROL)
                           www.carol.co.uk

Corporate Location www.corporatelocation.com
Economist Intelligence Unit www.eiu.com
Emerging Markets Companion www.emgmkts.com
Hieros Gamos/Lex Mundi Business Guides
 www.hg.org/guides.html
HUGIN www.huginonline.com
International Monetary Fund (IMF)
 www.imf.org
The Internationalist www.internationalist.com
Statistical data locators www.ntu.edu.sg/library/stat/
 statdata.htm
Trade Partners www.tradepartners.gov.uk

finding mailing lists

Mailing lists are a great way to keep up to date with colleagues or people interested in a specialist topic. With tens of thousands to choose from, you'll need to use one of these search engines to help you find the right one for your interests:

CataList www.lsoft.com/lists/listref.html
Liszt www.liszt.com
Tile.net www.tile.net

discussion groups and chat forums

Do you want to discuss marketing, business or E-commerce with other colleagues and professionals? Here are some of the best known E-business and marketing discussion groups. Alternatively, you could use a search engine such as Talkway (www.talkway.com) or Forum One (www.forumone.com).

- About.com · · · · · · · · · www.entrepreneurs.about.com
- Association for International Business
  www.profunda.dk/resources/
  business/aib.html
- Business 2.0 · · · · · · · · · www.business2.com
- Excite Chat · · · · · · · · · www.excite.com
- Fast Company · · · · · · · · www.fastcompany.com
- Guru.com · · · · · · · · · · www.guru.com
- Harvard Business School ListServs
  www.hbsp.harvard.edu/listservs/
  index.html
- International Trade · · · · · www.intl-trade.com/wwwboard/
- LinkExchange · · · · · · · · www.bcentral.com
- mail-list.com · · · · · · · · www.mail-list.com
- Private Equity Network · · · www.nvst.com
- PR Millions · · · · · · · · · www.free-publicity.com
- Red Herring · · · · · · · · · www.redherring.com
- Startup Network · · · · · · · www.delphi.com/
  startupnetwork/start/
- Yahoo! Business and Finance
  http://messages.yahoo.com/
  yahoo/business_and_finance/
- Wired · · · · · · · · · · · · www.wired.com
- Women Entrepreneurs Online Network
  www.weon.com

exhibitions and conventions

Do you need to find out if there are any conventions where you should be exhibiting? Here are specialist directories that attempt to list the shows in different countries and fields:

- Association for Conferences and Events · · · www.martex.co.uk/
  ace/
- Celebrity Speakers International · · · · · · · www.speakers.co.uk

▨ Exhibit Connections   www.exhibit-connections.com

▨ Exhibitions and Displays Direct   www.exhibitions-displays.co.uk

▨ Exhibitions Round the World   www.exhibitions-world.com

▨ Expobase   www.expobase.com
▨ EXPOweb   www.expoweb.com
▨ The Trade Group   www.tradegroup.com

▨ Venue Directory   www.venuedirectory.com

▨ Yahoo! Conventions and Trade Shows   uk.dir.yahoo.com/Business_and_Economy/Companies/Conventions_and Trade Shows/

promotional materials

Do you want a personalised balloon or a monogrammed diary gift? Marketing promotional material manufacturers have moved on to the Web – many offer their catalogue, some let you order online.

▨ Accolade   www.accolade.uk.com
▨ B-Loony balloons   www.b-loony.co.uk
▨ Castelli Diaries   www.castelli.co.uk
▨ Lancewich stress relievers   www.stress-relievers.com
▨ Mousemats   www.mousemats-r-us.com
▨ Pukka Promotions   www.netcomuk.co.uk/~pukka/promotion.html
▨ Sonata Business Gifts   www.sonata.co.uk/sbenter.html

▓ Yahoo! Promotional Items   uk.dir.yahoo.com/
        Business_and_Economy/
        Companies/
        Marketing_and_Advertising/
        Advertising/
        Promotional_Items/

e-mail software

E-mail software is dominated by the products that come as part of your Web browser – both Netscape and Microsoft supply excellent e-mail programs as part of the bundle. If you want to change to another, here are three free programs to download and try out:

▓ Eudora   www.qualcomm.com
▓ Outlook Express   www.microsoft.com
▓ Pegasus   www.pegasus.usa.com

free e-mail accounts

Almost every major website now seems to offer visitors a free e-mail address. These are a good way of separating personal and professional mail, accessing your mail when travelling, or as a dummy address when posting messages to newsgroups or discussion forums. Most only let you access your messages via an often slow and ad-filled website.

▓ Bigfoot   www.bigfoot.com
▓ Cometmail   www.cometmail.com
▓ Excite   www.excite.com
▓ Hotmail   www.hotmail.com
▓ Yahoo!   mail.yahoo.com

finding an e-mail address

If you're trying to find someone's e-mail address, you might find it tougher than you would expect. There's no central complete e-mail directory yet, but you could try looking in these separate directories, each of which covers some users:

- AltaVista   www.altavista.com
- BigFoot   www.bigfoot.com
- Excite   www.excite.com
- Who Where?   www.whowhere.com
- Yahoo! People Search   people.yahoo.com

newsgroup readers

Both major Web browsers from Microsoft and Netscape include a good newsgroup reader. However, if you fancy a change, here are some of the main stand-alone alternatives:

- Agent   www.forteinc.com
- Hogwasher   www.asar.com
- News Rover   www.newsrover.com
- NewsWatcher   www.download.com
- Outlook Express   www.microsoft.com
- Xnews   www.download.com

finding and searching newsgroups

Do you want to search the archives of a newsgroup to see what was posted months ago? Or do you simply need to find a newsgroup that matches your requirements? Use one of these specialist search tools. If you're still not sure about newsgroups, try the question-and-answer site for newsgroups, FAQ (www.faqs.org).

- Deja   www.deja.com
- Newsgroup Directory   tile.net/news
- Usenet Info Center   http://metalab.unc.edu/usenet-i/

management and filter software

Do you want to limit the places your colleagues visit on the Net? Or do you need to ensure that your company doesn't get sued for malicious, offensive or libellous e-mail messages? Use one of these Web filter products or Net management tools that will keep an eye on what everyone's doing:

- CyberPatrol   www.cyberpatrol.com
- CYBERsitter   www.cybersitter.com
- Mail essentials   www.gficomms.com
- Mailwall and Desktop Surveillance   www.omniquad.com
- MIMEsweeper   www.nha.com
- Net Nanny   www.netnanny.com
- SurfWatch   www.surfwatch.com

anti-virus software

Ensure that your computer, the files you download and e-mail attachments are free of malicious viruses by installing a special anti-virus program that will automatically check all new files. Don't forget, that new viruses are always being developed, so you'll need to download update files for your anti-virus software on a regular basis. Here are some of the main anti-virus products and companies:

McAfee	www.mcafee.com
Net Paradox	www.netparadox.com
NHA	www.nha.com
Norton AntiVirus	www.symantec.com
Omniquad	www.omniquad.com

glossary

access log   a record of every visitor to your website, together with details of when they visited and which pages they viewed. This log file is created automatically (just ask your ISP or hosting company to switch on the feature); use the results to see who visits when and which pages are most popular. If you set up special pages for ad response, it's easy to check the success of the campaign.

access provider   see *ISP*.

address (e-mail)   the unique name that identifies a particular person or account (a temporary store) for messages. For example, a unique personal e-mail address would be 'simon@workingsite.com'.

address (website)   the unique set of words (or numbers) that identifies the location of a website on the World Wide Web, sometimes called a *URL* (uniform resource locator). For example, 'www.workingsite.com' and 'www.microsoft.com' are two unique website addresses.

address book   a feature of an e-mail program that lets you store a list of contacts with their e-mail addresses.

ADSL   asymmetric digital subscriber line. The latest high-speed system for connecting to the Internet – several times faster than ISDN – but at a fixed, flat monthly subscription that has no per-minute call charges. In the UK, British Telecom's ADSL scheme is called OpenWorld (www.bt.com/openworld) and other ISPs are starting to offer the service at around £40 per month.

anti-virus program   special software that will check all the files on your hard disk to detect and remove viruses from program and document files. Always use anti-virus software to check any new file you download from the Internet or receive as an attachment via e-mail.

applet   a small program that is downloaded from a website and runs within your Web browser. Often used to provide special multimedia effects or for some shopping-cart systems.

attachment   one or more files (such as a document or spreadsheet) sent with an e-mail message.

authentication   a system that allows a company to prove that it is who it claims to be. The system is used to set up secure websites (see *SSL*) and uses a unique electronic certificate issued by independent certifiers to the company. The independent certifiers include VeriSign (www.verisign.com) and Thawte (www.thawte.com).

banner ad   the wide, oblong-shaped advertising panels that appear on just about every commercial website. Banner ads advertise a product, service or website and entice users to click on them and jump to the advertiser's website. See also *click-through* and *impression*.

bookmark   a feature of Web browser software that lets you store the address and description of a website in an address book within the browser. When you want to revisit the site, just select the bookmark entry. Microsoft calls this feature 'Favorites'.

bounce   this is when an e-mail message cannot be delivered and so has been returned to the sender. Sometimes this is because of a problem with the connection or the server, but is usually because the e-mail address is wrong.

certificate a unique set of numbers issued to a company as proof that it is who it claims to be. The certificate is generated by an independent trusted organisation (the two biggest are VeriSign and Thawte) once the company has satisfied the certifier that it is legitimate. The company needs this certificate to install a secure website feature (see *SSL*), normally used on a shopping or commerce site.

CGI common gateway interface. A system that lets a webpage send information to a program running on the server; used with specialist programs written to add features to a website. For example, if you want to add a search feature or discussion group, the program that carries out the function transfers information to the webpage using CGI. The programs are normally written in the *Perl* language.

click-through a measure of the number of viewers that click on a banner advert (and so jump to the advertiser's website). Used as a way of charging the advertiser for the advert. A click-through rate of just a few per cent is common. Most advertisers have to pay per impression – a less attractive scheme than paying per click-through (where you effectively pay for results).

cookie a tiny file stored on your computer by a website. The file can contain information such as your user name at the site, when you last visited or the last item you purchased. Sometimes vilified, but normally harmless and usually required for a shopping site to work at all.

CPA cost per action. The cost of one impression (the action of displaying a banner ad).

CTR click-through rate. The cost of one click-through for a banner ad. It's not very common to see ad rates displayed in this format (where you pay for results), instead it's more usual to pay a CPA rate.

database a collection of organised information that can be stored, searched and displayed – for example, your company's range of products, the office telephone directory or an encyclopaedia. Adding a database to your website can be a big draw for visitors – if the content is worth searching for! However, it can be complex to add a database, although new software such as Microsoft Front-Page and FileMaker both provide relatively simple routes to publishing online. The traditional route is to use a custom-written program or, for vast complex systems (such as details of all the books available at a bookshop), a specialist commercial product, such as Oracle, is often used.

digital certificate See *certificate.*

directory a website that contains a list of links to other websites, usually arranged in sections and often with a search feature. Yahoo! (www.yahoo.com) is one of the best-known directories and lists half a million websites. Search engines, such as Excite and AltaVista, take a different approach and try to include every website on the Net; directories are more selective.

DNS (domain name system) a method of converting a domain name to the numerical IP (Internet protocol) address that is used to locate the computer within the Internet. The vast table of domain names and their IP addresses are stored on a domain name server (also called DNS). For example, if you type in the domain name 'www.microsoft.com' in your Web browser, this is passed to a DNS that translates the name to a set of numbers that points to the location of the Microsoft server computer.

domain name a unique name that is used to identify one site (or server computer) on the Internet. For example, the domain name 'microsoft.com' identifies Microsoft's main server that supports its website (with the address www.microsoft.com) and its e-mail system.

download   to transfer information, usually a file, from a distant computer on to your own, usually via the Internet.

encryption   a system that can scramble text so that only the intended recipient can unscramble it and read it, protecting it against unauthorised viewing during its journey to the recipient.

FAQ   frequently asked question. List of, unsurprisingly, frequently asked questions and their answers. Most technical support sites provide a FAQ page to answer obvious and common questions.

firewall   a security system that protects a company's network of computers from access by hackers outside the company. If you plan to link your company's network to the Internet, make sure that you also install a firewall to provide basic security measures against unwanted attention from outside the company.

folder   a container for your e-mail messages within an e-mail program or, on a hard disk, a container for files.

forward   to send a message you have received on to another user.

freeware   software that can be used on a permanent basis without charge. Compare with *shareware*.

gateway   a link between two different types of system. For example, an e-mail–fax gateway converts e-mail messages to the correct fax format, then resends them to a fax machine.

geotargeting   a way of analysing and deducing where a website visitor is from or which location they are interested in, then displaying customised messages or advertisements. For example, if they ask for the weather in Seattle, you could display adverts from taxi companies in Seattle.

GIF a graphics file format used to store images – one of two popular ways of storing graphics for a webpage. See also *JPEG*.

hit technically, a request from a user's browser to view a particular page or image on your website. Often misleadingly used as a measure of the popularity of a website or a measure of the number of visitors – it could, after careful processing, provide some of this information, but you would need to analyse your site's access log files to find these details. The problem occurs because as each element within a webpage is displayed, it generates a 'hit'. If your home page has three pictures and some text, every user will generate four hits in your access log. If they click on the refresh button on their browser, another four hits are recorded, just for one visitor.

home page the initial page that's displayed when you visit a website. The home page is normally stored in a file called 'index. html'. If you type in the website address 'www.bbc.co.uk', you'll automatically see the BBC home page on its website.

host provider see *Web space provider*.

HTML hypertext markup language. The codes and commands that are used to define and format a webpage. These commands let you define the colour, style and position of text, links and images within the page.

HTTP hypertext transfer protocol. The way in which a Web browser talks to a Web server to request information. Actually a series of commands used by a browser to ask the Web server to transfer a particular page. Almost every full Web address (the URL) starts with these letters to tell the browser that you are typing in the address of a webpage, not an e-mail message or file transfer, which both use related protocols.

hyperlink (in HTML) a way of linking the address of a webpage to a word, picture or icon so that when you click on the word or object, you move to the new webpage. Hyperlinks are the building blocks of the Web and let you browse across pages.

hypertext a way of linking together webpages over the Web. One word or section of text, or even an image on a webpage, can be linked (this facility is often called a hyperlink) to jump to any other Web address on the site or on another website. When the user clicks on the link, they'll see the referenced page displayed. This is the system that lets you browse the Web.

impression the act of displaying a banner advertisement to a visitor on your website. If you want to pay for a banner ad to be displayed, you will probably be charged per impression. Typical rates are from \$50–\$200 per thousand impressions.

Internet or Net the millions of computers that are linked together around the world, allowing any computer to communicate with any other that is part of the network.

intranet a mini, private Internet that's only accessible to users on a company's internal network.

ISDN integrated services digital network. A high-speed digital version of your standard phone line. You'll get a speedy connection to the Internet using an ISDN link, but you need a special modem (called a terminal adapter) and an ISP that provides ISDN access for its users. ISDN is being overtaken by cable modems and ADSL technology.

ISP Internet service provider. A company that provides users with a link to the Internet. You need to subscribe (sometimes for free) and in return you get a user name, a password and a telephone access number that your modem can dial to link to the Internet.

Javascript   programming language that lets webpage designers enhance the basic effects provided by HTML.

JPEG   a graphics file format used to store images – often used to store photographic or high-quality images that can be displayed on a website.

key word   a word that you type in at a search engine to help you find relevant information.

link   see *hypertext*.

List server   See *mailing list*.

log analysis   special software that converts the raw data recorded automatically each time a visitor looks at your website into graphs or tables that let you see clearly information such as how many visitors view the site and which pages are most popular.

logfile   see *access log*.

mailing list   efficient, simple method of distributing information to a wide group of people who all share a common interest. The mailing list is simply a collection of e-mail addresses stored in a file; any message sent to the mailing list is automatically re-distributed to all the users on the list. There are tens of thousands of mailing lists covering just about every possible subject area; to find something relevant, search www.liszt.com.

mail server   a computer on the Internet that manages and distributes e-mail messages, ensuring that they are sent to the correct location.

meta-tags   special information included at the top of the file that contains a webpage's HTML commands and is used to help a search engine correctly index and summarise the contents of the page. By creating meta-tags, you are helping direct the search engine's indexing process to point towards the relevant or interesting features of your site.

modem   a device that links your computer to a telephone line and allows you to dial into an ISP – and so connect to the Internet. A modem (*mo*dulator/*dem*odulator) converts your computer's data into sound signals that can be sent along a phone line.

newsgroup   a public discussion forum where just about anything can be said. There are over 60 000 individual newsgroups on the net (collectively called Usenet), each covering a particular subject or area of interest.

newsreader   special software that lets you view and participate in a newsgroup; almost all current Web browsers include a newsreader feature.

offline   not connected to the Internet

online   connected to the Internet.

opt-in mailing list   a mailing list of e-mail addresses in which each person has agreed to receive advertising or marketing e-mail messages about a particular subject. If you rent an e-mail mailing list, make sure that it's an opt-in list.

page impression   a measure of how many times a webpage has been displayed to visitors. Often used as a crude way of counting the visitors to a site. See also *impression*.

page requests   a measure of the number of pages that visitors have viewed in a day. Often used as a crude way of indicating the popularity of your website. See also *log analysis*.

Perl   a programming language that's particularly popular with developers creating custom applications for websites. Almost every commercial ISP (but not usually the free ISPs) lets you write your own Perl programs to add a discussion group, shopping cart or chat session to your website.

PGP   pretty good privacy. An encryption system that is very se-cure and is a popular way of encrypting e-mail or a file so that only the intended recipient can decrypt and read the information.

post office   see *mail server*.

privacy statement   a document included on your website that defines your company's policy regarding what it will (and hope-fully will not) do with any personal information collected from visitors – such as their names and addresses submitted when or-dering goods.

public domain   text, images or software that is freely available to anyone to view and use, but not to resell. The copyright remains with the original author.

secure site   a section of a website that implements a system (al-most always the SSL system) to provide a secure channel between the website and your browser, ensuring that anything you type in (such as your credit card details) cannot be read by a hacker.

server access log   see access log

shareware   software that can be used for a certain period (often a month) to try it out, before you have to pay for it.

shopping cart/basket   the electronic equivalent of a trolley that you would use in a supermarket. As you browse around an online shopping website, you can add products you want to buy to your shopping cart then, when you've finished, you pay for the goods by typing in your credit card details.

signature   (i) (on a secure website) a unique authentication code that identifies a company as part of its authentication certificate;

(ii) (in an e-mail) the lines of text that are automatically added to the end of any e-mail you write (or newsgroup message that you post) and normally include your name, company name, slogan and basic contact details.

spam an unwanted e-mail message sent in bulk to thousands of addresses to try to advertise something. Also refers to an advertising message posted to dozens of newsgroups at a time.

SSL Secure Sockets Layer. A system that scrambles the data between your Web browser and the website, so providing a secure channel. Used to create a secure section of a website where you can safely type in personal or credit card details. Your browser indicates that you are using a secure SSL page by displaying a tiny closed padlock icon in the bottom status bar.

unsolicited mail advertising e-mail that you have not requested, often called *spam*.

URL uniform resource locator. The correct term for the full address of a webpage. For example, 'bbc.co.uk' is a domain name, 'www.bbc.co.uk' is the website address for the BBC and 'www.bbc.co.uk/index.html' is the URL to the site's home page.

Usenet see *newsgroup*.

web browser software that lets you view a webpage and navigate through the Web. The latest Web browser software (from Microsoft and Netscape) also includes an e-mail program and a news reader.

web page a single, discrete page within a website. Individual webpages are stored in separate files that contain the HTML commands describing the layout of the page.

Web server a computer that stores all the pages and images and other material that together form a website. Generally, Web servers store hundreds of separate websites or, in the case of mammoth sites from the BBC or CNN, several computers are used to store the website.

website a collection of webpages that together provide information about a particular product, person or company.

Web space provider a company that rents out Web space on its Web server computers where you can store the elements that form your website. Most ISPs provide you with Web space in return for your subscription.

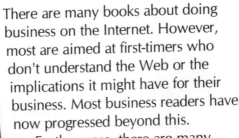

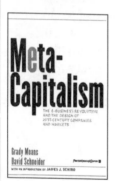